ESSENCE OF A COMPETENT MANAGER

S.K. TARAFDER

ATLANTIC
PUBLISHERS & DISTRIBUTORS

Published by
ATLANTIC PUBLISHERS AND DISTRIBUTORS
B-2, Vishal Enclave, Opp. Rajouri Garden, New Delhi-110027
Phones : 25413460, 25429987, 25466842

Sales Office
7/22, Ansari Road, Darya Ganj, New Delhi-110002
Phones : 23273880, 23275880, 23280451
Fax : 91-11-23285873
web : www.atlanticbooks.com
e-mail : info@atlanticbooks.com

ISBN 81-269-0381-3

Printed in India at
Nice Printing Press, Delhi

Preface

Managers are the pillars of organisations. Although they are working in an independent capacity, they are no doubt instrumental in the hands of the highest echelon of the management as far as policy matters are concerned to run establishments with efficiency in pursuance of their directives and guidance. With the privatisation policy of the government of India, number of organisations under the management of private ownership are on the increase and in order to run such organisations to the zenith of efficiency, competent Managers are the need of the day.

This book titled, *Essence of A Competent Manager*, will prove to be a very useful for the Managers who are already working and also for those who have the innate inclination to become Managers of organisations in their future career. The book has dwelt with practical aspects on a number of matters which the Managers ought to know in order to fertilise their working with utmost efficiency and zeal. Efficient Managers are the crying need of the day and that they will derive maximum benefits to enrich their knowledge of working through perusal of this book. By virtue of my practical experience which I gained by working in senior managerial capacity for sixteen years with the organisations of All-India repute, I have given pragmatic views for the benefits of the Managers who have the absolute desire to be fully successful in their working. Through questions and answers I have also discussed many important issues which the persons working in managerial capacity have to know in their own interest to work with credibility.

Apart from the Administrative Managers, the book will be very useful for the Personnel Managers who are required to deal with multifarious problems in their day-to-day working in personnel matters. Through answers to the questions many aspects of personnel matters have been highlighted in befitting manners which will give extensive knowledge to the Personnel Managers in the discharge of their duties and that they will feel plain sailing in dealing with personnel matters.

Throughout the book, I have used masculine gender, such as 'He/Manager' without mentioning the feminine gender, such as 'She/Manageress' in juxtaposition with the masculine gender. While I beg apology from the female readers of this book for not mentioning feminine gender, I have used the masculine gender only for the purpose of ease in writing.

S.K. TARAFDER

CONTENTS

1
Who are Managers?

Customary definition of Manager is that the person who acts to manage the affairs of the organisation is a Manager. Managers of organisations have to instil in them the managerial qualities needed to justify performance of official duties in consonance with their designation. Excellent Managers are those who prove equal to the task. Managers are the inviolable and solid pillars of organisations on which depend the prosperity of the establishments where they work. Competent Managers are the essence of rejuvenating the economic morbidity of the establishments steering clear the obstacles standing in the way of development of such organisations. While efficient running of organisations stimulates generation of employment potentiality, Managers have to play a great role in solving unemployment problem by making the organisations economically viable by their indefatigable working.

Needless to elucidate, country's development depends largely upon the efficient Managers who are the guiding force to mould the economy of the country to the betterment by way of efficient running of organisations, which is the absolute need of the day. Managers have to realise always that they are engaged not only for the sake of normal discharge of their duties but also for broader perspective and that they have immense and perennial responsibilities to shoulder being placed in Managerial position.

Managers must have creative instincts with a managerial perspective and skill. There won't also be any dearth of expert advice from them. Managers should be acquainted with organisational behaviour. They should also need to deal with the time orientation of employees as they attempt to compete through speed. The temporal perspective work-teams become an important issue for the Manager to bear in mind when cooperation among several departments is required or is essential for performance of tasks. Also the Managers cannot ignore the human element while managing a company.

The following chapters have elaborately dealt with the aspects as to how to become a successful Manager. "Success is the progressive realization of a worthy goal"—says Earl Nightingale.

2

PERSONALITY OF A MANAGER

A Manager must possess personality. It is one of the most important factors on which depends upon the success of a Manager. Personality is an essential ingredient needed to be maintained by a successful Manager throughout the entire period of his service career. Personality does not mean that a Manager is essentially required to be good looking which alone will not suffice the purpose entirely. Appearance in fact is considered to determine personality of a Manager. When a Manager has to work in the office along with his co-officers and subordinate staff members, his personality will go a long way in maintaining rapprochement with them in the interest of smooth working and here lies the success of a Manager. A Manager with personality is liked by everybody who feels closed to him. This is his added qualification in the discharge of his duties efficiently in communion with them. Now, after discussing in the foregoing all about the personality, the question naturally crops up what are the traits of personality. Personality is the embodiment of the following traits:

(i) Self-confidence

(ii) Fixity of mind

(iii) Capacity to influence others

(iv) Clarity of expression

(v) Not to be fickle minded

(vi) Capacity of quick understanding

(vii) Wearing of well fitted costume

(viii) Positive approach on matters

(ix) Cleanliness
(x) Gravity
(xi) Steadiness in walking
(xii) Sense of etiquette
(xiii) Good manners
(xiv) Will power
(xv) Gentleness
(xvi) Soft spoken
(xvii) Cool temperament
(xviii) Good behaviour
(xix) Loveable habits

Explanations of the above traits seriatim are the following:

Self-Confidence

Since a Manager has to shoulder higher responsibilities in the discharge of his duties, he should have self-confidence for attaining perfection in the job he does. Therefore, for a successful Manager, self-confidence is an absolute necessity.

Fixity of Mind

A Manager has to take multifarious decisions in the interest of the organisation he serves. Therefore, he has to think twice before arriving at a final decision. Otherwise, it may be detrimental to the interest of the organisation and the Manager taking such decision will be held entirely responsible for the same. Hence, fixity of mind of a successful Manager is a prerequisite so as to avoid swinging of decisions which will speak of the unsteady mind of the Manager. Unsteady mind is a disqualification to become a successful Manager.

Capacity to Influence Others

Getting jobs done by influencing others is the yardstick of a successful Manager. For attaining this art he is to be amiable in disposition. Choleric disposition of the Manager will ruffle others and the jobs cannot be got done by him by influencing them. This will be his disqualification and will go against his personality. Therefore, a Manager has to cultivate the art of influencing others.

Clarity of Expression

Clarity of expression is a part of personality of a Manager. With clarity of expression of the Manager the employees do not feel confused to understand things he explains to them and the jobs are done by them efficiently and without error.

Not to be Fickle Minded

Fickle mindedness is a great weakness of a Manager. With fickle mindedness the employees do not in fact treat him with respect and when respectability is wanting discipline in the organisation cannot be upheld. Higher management will also try to get rid of such fickle minded Manager.

Capacity of Quick Understanding

One of the ingredients of a successful Manager is that he should have the capacity of quick understanding of things which will help him perform his duties with promptitude and dexterity. Quick understanding of things will also conduce him to work against time thus instilling efficiency in the working of the Manager.

Wearing of Well Fitted Costume

A Manager must be well dressed. This will enhance Company's prestige. Wearing of well fitted costume with proper dressing of hair brings smartness which reflects in the working.

Positive Approach on Matters

A successful Manager is a person who has positive approach on matters. Negative approach retards progress of work and the work of the Manager goes on piling up for such negative approach and ultimately he becomes a failure in the discharge of his duties.

Cleanliness

Propensity for inculcating cleanliness is a virtue. This brings perfection in the working of a Manager.

Gravity

Gravity is a very important part to become a successful Manager. Employees treat the Manager with gravity in high esteem.

Steadiness in Walking

Steadiness in walking by a Manager reflects the promptness of his action on every matter.

Sense of Etiquette

A Manager must have sense of etiquette. It proves elegance of his mind which otherwise means that he is a man of good taste. Elegance and highness of mind is the essence of a successful Manager.

Good Manners

A Manager possessing good manners is a person hailing from aristocratic family. Successful Managers are those who come of respectable families. Family background is very important for a person to become a Manager because his attitude is moulded on the basis of his family environment.

Will Power

A Manager having will power is indomitable and such indomitable Manager is a strong pillar for the organisation, who can face any ordeal bravely and successfully that may come during the course of his working. His will power will help him acquire further higher position in the organisation.

Gentleness

The essence of a successful Manager is gentleness. His gentle habits make him loveable amongst the employees.

Soft Spoken

A successful Manager must be soft spoken. Speaking in loud voice by a Manager disturbs others in their working and also it does not speak high of the Manager. Well polished Manager is always soft spoken. When a Manager is soft spoken, others will also follow suit and the company's work continues in peaceful atmosphere. Pandemonium is contradictory to peaceful working.

Cool Temperament

A successful Manager must have cool temperament always. Since he is saddled with plenty of work at his disposal, it is essentially desired that his cool temperament will go a long way in solving the knotty problems. A Manager with ruffled temperament complicates matters and the company has to suffer a lot for his immature decision which owes for his intemperance. Therefore, cool temperament is the essence of a successful Manager.

Good Behaviour

Devotion to duties by the employees is the result of good behaviour of the Manager. It is the psychological effect of good behaviour of the Manager that the employees are inspired to do more work without whiling away their time. By this way, the company gets benefit arising out of the increased output of work performed by the employees.

Loveable Habits

Loveable habits of the Manager draw the employees closer to him in the discharge of duties. Extraction of work from the employees by showing red eyes is primitive. Work through love and affection as shown by the Manager is the go of the modern times. By such way of working formation of union in the organisation is also a remote possibility.

It is, therefore, of prime importance that a Manager desiring to be successful in his working, the above traits are absolutely indispensable for application.

3

Responsibility of a Manager

Under no circumstances, a Manager can shirk off his responsibilities in the discharge of his duties. There is a saying, "Responsibilities gravitate to the person who can shoulder them". When a Manager accepts responsibility he is actually giving himself promotion. A Manager who is away from shouldering responsibilities is of course not set free from being responsible. When he thinks himself responsible he can take judicious actions during the course of his working. Responsibility involves thoughtful action. There is maturity of thoughts and actions of a Manager when he is responsible in his behaviour. It is the general tendency of human being that when things go wrong he does not want to accept responsibility. But, when things go right he takes the credit whether he has taken responsibility for the same or not. But, in the case of a Manager this should not be made applicable. He must be bold to accept that he is responsible for things going wrong and here lies his credibility. By this, the higher management of the organisation will not nurture the opinion that such a Manager is an opportunist and at the same time he will enjoy respectability from all for his bold confession of folly. A responsible Manager is no doubt a successful and trustworthy Manager. The price of greatness is responsibility. Shouldering responsibility by a Manager is his moral obligation.

Effect of Responsibility of a Manager on the Employees

The effect of his being responsible is that the subordinate employees can learn from him as to how they have to cultivate the habit of generating sense of responsibility which will pave the way for their future prosperity in service. Irresponsibility of a person is a degeneration. An irresponsible

Manager cannot have control over his staff members, because he cannot remain firm and steady in the eye of the employees and consequently they do not discharge their duties with care and responsibility taking cue of the irresponsibility of their Manager. A responsible Manager is a strong pillar of an organisation. The employees will feel elated when they work under a responsible Manager. Responsibility brings discipline. The employees are made disciplined when they work through discipline which is the aftermath of the responsible way of working of the Manager under whom they work. Instances are plenty that many employees have ascended the ladder of higher position in service because of the high degree of training they received by virtue of their working under a competent and responsible Manager and this has become their asset throughout the entire period of their service career.

4

INSTILLING TEAM SPIRIT AND DEVELOPING MOTIVATION AMONGST THE EMPLOYEES

One of the factors determining the success of a Manager is how he is able to infuse team spirit and ignite motivation amongst the employees. Team work accentuates progress of work in an organisation. Work cannot be extracted from the employees by coercive methods adopted by a Manager. A Manager must take into account the performance of the working group (or team) which will have the effect of team spirit. This makes for greater accountability. It also encourages cooperation amongst co-workers. In the new dispensation, team players have the edge. Today, overall corporate performance is also a factor.

Apart from instilling team spirit a Manager has also to encourage generation of motivation by the employees which is very important to attain dexterity in the working of the organisation. Motivation means to turn on or ignite the feeling or action. Motivation is a driving force. It can persuade and propel the employees into action. In other words, motivation can be defined as motive for action. It is a force that can transform life.

Now, the question is can the Manager motivate the employees? The answer must be in the negation. The thing is that it is the employees who motivate themselves and not the others who can motivate them. A Manager has of course to inspire them to motivate themselves. He can create conducive environment which can be motivating. In order to inspire the employees to motivate themselves, a Manager has to understand their sentiments, needs and wants. The difference between inspiration and motivation is that inspiration is changing thinking; motivation is changing action.

Success of Manager will depend upon his taking the following actions and then only the employees will have sense of team spirit and motivation:

(a) A Manager should treat the employees in such a way that they are not made to feel that they have no status in the company,

(b) Human mind is very much sensitive. Therefore, a Manager should not hurt the sentiment of the employees by taking such action or talking with them in irrational way,

(c) He should treat all the employees with equal eyes. Feelings of nepotism and favouritism should not dawn in the minds of a Manager,

(d) He should have soft corner in his mind to understand the genuine problems and difficulties of the employees,

(e) Previously, the concept was master and servant relations in the office. But, now this concept has changed altogether as employee-employer relations. Although a Manager is a Management staff, yet his relations with the employees will be very sweet and cordial in view of the changed situation in modern day employment,

(f) A Manager at the same time should not show laxity while dealing with the erring employees, else his administration will fail and that he will be an unsuccessful Manager,

(g) He should listen to what the employees say,

(h) He should give recognition to the services of the employees.

While inspiring the employees to motivate themselves, a Manager should be well aware of what are the factors by which the employees are demotivated. They are:

(a) Unfair and negative criticism,

(b) Humiliation to the employees,

(c) Disregarding self-esteem to the employees,

(d) Bad office politics.

5

Academic Qualification of a Manager

Excellent academic qualification is not the absolute criterion to become a Manager of a Company. If we take into account that only those persons are eligible to become the Managers having high degree of academic education, it is a mistaken conception. Everybody is not fortunate to prosecute studies to acquire high degree of academic education because of multiple reasons, and it has been observed that such persons are also competent Managers. While it is an admitted fact that persons with excellent academic qualifications are eligible to become Managers by virtue of their harnessing with sufficient knowledge so acquired through such education, many persons have also managerial capability and competence with lesser academic qualification not equalising with those having high degree of academic qualification.

In this connexion, it will be appropriate to analyse what is education in true sense of the term. If any person has the ability to choose between wisdom and foolishness and between good and bad irrespective of academic degrees, they are called educated persons. Such educated persons can also become Managers having value based education, mental acumen and intelligence with which they are able to understand things quickly and sort out problems, whatever difficult the same may be.

Even without excellent academic qualification a person could be successful in his every effort if he is in possession of conviction, courage, courtesy, character and commitment. Many of the Managers must have all the above principles even when they are not highly educated academically.

Intelligence and ability are also other traits of a person facilitating him to become a Manager although he may not have high degree of academic qualification. Intelligence helps quicken to learn and ability is the skill to apply what is learnt. Knowledge is something which can also be acquired without high degree of academic qualification, and this knowledge could be fully utilised by the Manager during the course of his working. Knowledge is information which is a potential power and this power is the most essential power required by a Manager.

From the above analyses it is construed that high degree of academic qualification is not necessarily required in all the cases to become a successful Manager in a Company provided he can develop the required traits to work as Manager. There is of course no denying the fact that the highly educated persons with speciality in commercial and management degrees are by far competent to become Managers and the importance of such persons in commercial world is immense.

6

COURTESY AND MANNERS

Success of a person depends upon courtesy and manners. Instances are plenty that many talented persons have failed to attain their own success because they are derelict of courtesy and manners. A man of courtesy and manners is a man of refined temperament and politeness which are the hallmark of gentleness. Courtesy and good manners enhance the self-growth of a person. It costs nothing to be courteous but pays a lot not only to the individual but to the organisation too. A man of courtesy and good manners is loveable by all and sundry. He does not have any foe. A man of towering personality is one endowed with the virtue of courtesy and manners. Such person is elevated in the eye of others.

A Manager in an organisation must be a person of qualities. When one of the qualities of a person is adjudged by his courtesy and manners it is of paramount necessity that a Manager must be a person of courtesy and manners. Otherwise, his success as Manager will have retrograde step. While a Manager without courtesy and manners is not liked by others, he will not be able to imprint good impressions in the minds of the officials/executives of other organisations also and that he will find it difficult to get the job done of which he is entrusted with.

Gentleness and politeness of a Manager enhance the prestige, honour and reputation of the organisation where he serves. A Manager with ruffled and choleric disposition is derelict of courtesy and manners which is his negative point to become a Manager. Good manners and courteous behaviour of a Manager bring the employees close to him which is very much conducive to generate team spirit in working. This obviously leads to prosperity of the organisation in the long run.

Manager's contribution is immense for the well-being of an organisation when he is a person of courtesy and manners which play an important part for him to become a successful Manager. Job of a Manager is as such that he has to face many obstacles and ordeals during the course of his working. His success is measured in terms when he has done the jobs well by overcoming the impediments. He will of course feel plain sailing in getting success in his jobs when he will be assisted by his employees and co-officers in most of the cases because of his amiable and loveable habits which he has acquired by his courtesy and manners.

7

Leadership Qualities of a Manager

Everybody cannot be a responsible and successful Manager unless otherwise he has the leadership qualities. If a person has strong inclination to rise high in service he can think of developing leadership qualities. Leadership qualities drive a person to reach the highest echelon of life. It all depends upon how a person is enthusiastic. Enthusiasm breeds a person to become energetic. A successful Manager must be energetic. In all the cases, leadership qualities are not inborn. The leadership qualities of a Manager are:

(a) He should have sound knowledge of work,

(b) He should distribute work in such a way that the employees are not overburdened, otherwise the work cannot be done by them with perfection,

(c) All the employees should be made to feel that they are part and parcel of the organisation,

(d) He should treat all the employees with equal eyes,

(e) He must have patience,

(f) He should not utter any unparliamentary words which will injure the hearts of the employees,

(g) He should have good rapprochement with other officers of the company,

(h) He should be bold enough to take decision,

(i) He should discipline the employees,

(j) He should encourage the employees,

(k) He should not lose temper on any occasion,

(1) He should listen to what the subordinates say and try to solve their problems,

(m) There should not be any sense of favouritism in him,

(n) He should not criticise any employee,

(o) He should have the capability to study the behavioural pattern and psychology of the employees,

(p) He should maintain cordial relations with the employees,

(q) He must maintain punctuality in attending office to set example for others,

(r) He should not tolerate any laxity in the performance to work by the employees,

(s) He should understand and realise the genuine difficulties and problems of the employees,

(t) He should have fore-sightedness *i.e.*, he must conjecture what may be the repercussion after he takes action on any matter, because every action has reaction.

8

Prompt Disposal of Paper Work

Efficiency of a Manager is manifested through his quick disposal of papers/letters. Paper work is one of the important functions of a Manager. If a Manager is weak in disposal of papers/ letters he cannot be considered as a competent and successful Manager. There are of course reasons as to why a Manager takes dilatory action in dealing with the paper work which may be—either he is oscillating to take firm decision on matters of importance or he is devoid of conception to deal with matters. On account of dilatory process to deal with the paper work for the probable reasons as adduced above, there is deluge of huge papers on his desk and under this situation a Manager is totally confused what to do and it becomes an up-hill task for him to overcome the impasse.

A Manager must always bear in mind that paper work is not the only part of his entire work but he has to make use of his valuable time to attend to other matters of importance also. Therefore, if a Manager has to devote his attention to face the spate of paper work only, he cannot do justice to the organisation as a Manager by his working. A Manager is no doubt a great expectation of the organisation. Paper work is not the only expectation of him by the higher management.

Now, the question arises how to deal with the spate of paper work, especially in respect of correspondence. Conception of ideas is a very important factor to deal with the correspondence. Through correspondence mental acumen of the Manager is exhibited as also the Company's image is upheld. For speedy disposal of paper work a Manager has to earmark those letters of policy matters to be dealt with by him only. As far as disposal of other letters is concerned, his

PA/Assistant should be taken into confidence to draft out such letters.

By virtue of considerable period of his working in the organisation, a Manager must have thorough conception which will help him dispose of the letters of policy matters at the quickest possible time. Drafting knowledge of a Manager is also very important which will help quicken disposal of letters.

By following the above procedure to deal with the paper work, a Manager will get ample time to devote his attention in other matters and his competence and success in managerial capacity will be enhanced and he will be indispensable for the organisation he serves.

9

Trustworthiness

A successful Manager must be trustworthy in his actions, behaviour and character. For a Manager it is of utmost necessity that he has to maintain interactions with the Management at the helm of affairs and other employees of the organisation and this interaction is based on trust. The working of a Manager without interaction and trust is void and he cannot be taken into confidence by the higher Management. It is very important for a Manager to work in the organisation with honour and prestige by creating trust. Now, the crux of the question is how to build trust. The factors for building trust are:

(a) The Manager has to build confidence by his sincerity and honesty of working,

(b) He must have unblemished character,

(c) He should give due respect to the dignified persons of the higher Management,

(d) He must have consistency between his words and deeds,

(e) He must prove his competence and attitude to service,

(f) He must be a person of integrity,

(g) He must create impression that he is a person of reliability.

If a Manager has lost confidence in the higher Management, he cannot enjoy the laurels of his position and that he will always be a suspicious person. This is unbecoming of his managerial position in the organisation and his service career in such case will have a retrograde step. He will be considered unworthy of the position and the higher Management will think of getting rid of such Manager losing trust and confidence. Trustworthiness is a very important factor for a person working in higher position in any organisation.

A Manager has to know that following are the principal factors which cause distrust:

(a) Negative attitude,

(b) Lack of courtesy,

(c) Inconsistent and uncooperative behaviour,

(d) Lack of honesty and integrity,

(e) Selfishness,

(f) Clandestine tendency to extract money from the Company fraudulently.

Trust without integrity cannot be generated. A Manager must be a person of integrity if he has to maintain affinity and cordial relations with the higher Management by his trustworthiness. Therefore, a Manager has to think always that the trust he has created remains perpetual, as this will pave the way for further rise in his service career.

10

Not to Indulge in Loose Talks and Avoiding Criticism Aimed at the Employees

Sentiments of human beings are very much perceptible by sense. String of heart is very soft and touchy. It is extremely susceptible even at the slightest friction. Such being the circumstances, employees are to be treated with extreme caution and care. Since they have sense of respectability—no matter whether they may work in humble position, a Manager has to see that while dealing with them, their sentiments are not hurt by uttering loose talks. Otherwise, their minds will be tormented and it will affect the working of the organisation on account of resorting to go-slow tactic by the employees. If the Manager has to educate the employees to rectify their follies in working, they are to be educated not by shouting and showing red eyes but by words spiced with tenderness, love and affection. This in effect will motivate them and they will take extreme caution and care not to commit the same mistakes in their working in future. They will also hold the Manager with respectability. Talking in tender mindedness with the employees by the Manager does not in any way exhibit his weakness but highness of his mind. Therefore, a Manager should never indulge in loose talks with the employees. He should maintain gravity and control his tongue which will gravitate the employees towards him.

As far as the word, 'criticism' is concerned it is of two types—one is to criticise the person and the other is to criticise the working of the person. Criticism has also another distinguishing feature *i.e.*, positive criticism and negative criticism. It is always desirable that if one has to criticise the working of the person it should be constructive and not negative. Otherwise, he will be down-hearted and will lose inspiration to work with zeal and enthusiasm. It has also to be taken care of that while criticising self-esteem of the person is not hurt.

When the definition of criticism is as such that no employee should be criticised personally by the Manager, but his working, the Manager has to see that while indulging in positive criticism of the working of the employees it must have stimulating effect. Following are the ways as to how to criticise the working of the employees for the purpose of heightening motivation:

(a) In the criticism there should be full of suggestions for improving the working of the employees,

(b) While criticising, opportunity has to be given to explain the position of the employees,

(c) Criticism should centre round the benefits the employees have to derive by correcting their mistakes,

(d) Criticism should be made privately and not in presence of other employees,

(e) In the criticism there should not be words of intimidation,

(f) Criticism should be made with helping attitude,

(g) Criticism should not be ambiguous so as to avoid resentment in the minds of the employees,

(h) While criticising, the Manager is to be cool minded and firm.

Criticising the working of the employees in positive and constructive ways is very necessary in order to ensure mistake-free working. This will help the employees to be more cautious in their working in future. Hence, criticism made by the Manager should be taken by the employees in right perspective and also they should accept the same as benediction. Managers have to ensure that on no occasion they should criticise the employees personally but their performance. They should also offer solutions in their criticism.

11

A Manager should Listen to what the Employees say

One of the prerequisites of a Manager is not to throttle the sentiments and/or views which the employees want to give vent to, rather he should encourage them to speak to him with their own reasoning which may not even be acceptable. This will help the Manager to correct their wrong conceptions and the employees will feel enthused to know the unknown. This way the employees will find opportunity to develop their knowledge of working.

While listening to the employees the Manager has to see that:

(a) He should never speak more than listening,

(b) He should not interrupt when the employees are continuing to speak,

(c) He should give a patient hearing to the employees without being absent-minded,

(d) He should be a good listener in order to inspire the employees to express their views, as listening shows caring attitude of the Manager and the employees will feel more motivated,

(e) While listening he should avoid distractions,

(f) When the employees are speaking on a particular topic, the Manager should not change the subject of discussion,

(g) While listening he should show due respect and understanding,

(h) While the employees are speaking on a particular topic, they should be made to feel by the Manager that he is showing empathy,

(i) While listening the Manager should have eye contact with the employees.

By adhering to the above stratagems of listening to the employees by the Manager, this is also another way of creating situations by which the employees will feel motivated in their working and the success of a Manager will be manifested when the employees are motivated. What is needed most is that a Manager must have to draw asunder the barriers to effective listening. Enkindling enthusiasm in the minds of the employees is a part of function of a successful Manager and the creation of enthusiasm is the result of effective listening by the Manager. Enthusiasm inspires confidence and builds royalty to the Manager by the employees.

It is, therefore, incumbent on the part of the Manager to realise how effective it is to have a patient hearing to what the employees want to express. In this connexion, the Manager should also remember that he should not go on continuing to listen to the employees most of the time at the cost of his other work, for which he has to allot time for the employees.

12

Capacity to Surmise Reaction to the Action taken by a Manager

A Manager must have the capacity to surmise reaction to the action taken by him, because he must be well aware of the fact that every action has got reaction. Reckless and immature action taken by a Manager without conjecturing the complications which emanate out of the same will put him in awkward situation as also the Company where he serves. Moreover, for such immature action taken by him, his services with the Company may even be at stake. It is, therefore, of paramount necessity that a judicious Manager must think twice before taking a final action, so that the reaction to the same does not become detrimental to the interest of the organisation as also his position as Manager. A Manager is part and parcel of an organisation. His deeds and actions are very important in upholding the prestige of the organisation. Matured action taken by a Manager speaks high of his competence.

Since a Manager is one of the pillars of the organisation, he cannot shirk of his responsibilities to the organisation and being a responsible Manager he has to take action instantly at times of exigency of circumstances and in such case he has to be meticulous to take judicious action in the interest of the organisation on the basis of his mental make-up and maturity of thought so that such action does not have any adverse effect. If the Manager is swinging in his action it proves of his incompetence to work as Manager. Therefore, in order to become a competent and successful Manager he must be alert to take appropriate action on any matter and this will prove his capacity to surmise reaction to the action taken by him.

For the purpose of taking judicious action so that its reaction does not impair the prestige of the organisation, a Manager needs assessment of his risk-taking ability and in this connexion analyses of his strengths, weaknesses, opportunities and threats (SWOT) are essential.

13

KEEPING NORMALCY IN DEALING WITH SPATE OF WORK

Patience is a great quality and a moral excellence of a Manager, by virtue of which he can overcome problems volley after volley. A Manager has to pass through spate of work. But, he is not to be ruffled in dealing with such volumes of work. Otherwise there will not be any distinction between the working of a Manager and that of the non-managerial employees. Keeping normalcy in his temperament in dealing with the spate of work is very important which is essentially needed to work with efficiency and speed by a Manager. It requires strength of mind which is attained by devotion and practice.

The function of a Manager is variegated and not conventionalised. His mind has, therefore, to play in different ways in dealing with different nature of work and that too with maturity of thought. Maturity of thought is acquired through unruffled mind and practical experience. With cool brain and normal state of mind a successful Manager is required to sort out the intricacies of the problems. He will stumble at every stage if he becomes choleric in disposition in dealing with spate of work and thus he cannot win confidence in the higher management. A Manager cannot expect that he would be idling away in the office for insufficient work at his disposal but will be saddled with heaps of papers on his desk for disposal apart from doing other work of policy matters.

One important point is that keeping normalcy in dealing with spate of work, a Manager is essentially needed to be humourous and jovial which will exterminate his unsteady state of mind and he will find plain sailing in dealing with even the most complicated work. Success of a Manager is measured in terms of his steadiness and normalcy of mind at the time of dealing with the spate of work. But, at the same time his mind should not be diverted to other trifling matters when he is set to work of prime importance.

If a Manager is irked to find the volumes of work to be performed by him, disposal of the same will be procrastinated with the result that there will be continuous piling of work and it will go out of his capacity and control to deal with such voluminous work. He will then feel fish out of water and will be considered an inefficient Manager in the eye of the higher management.

Under the circumstances, a Manager must be firm, steady and normal in dealing with spate of work if he is to be a successful Manager in the organisation.

14

ESCHEWING THE HABIT OF BACK-BITING

A Manager must be clean-minded possessing moral integrity. He should not blow hot and cold in the same breadth. A Manager ought to know that drawing respects from others cannot be purchased. He may nurture the idea that by virtue of his position in the organisation employees would show their respects towards him. But, it is not a correct conception of a Manager. True respect comes from the core of heart. Showing outward respect is artificial. If a Manager is a dubious and a double standard person and also in the habit of back-biting, he as a Manager is not a sophisticated person in the eye of the employees and the higher management. Back-biting, if it is resorted to by a Manager, cannot pay him anything rather his position will be slandered. With such habit he will not be treated as a reliable person and the employees cannot expect of such Manager to do anything good for them. With back-biting tendency of a Manager even the position of an honest, sincere and hard working employee may be jeopardised in the eye of the higher management if such employee happens to be in sordid relation with the Manager for any unforeseen circumstances and even the services of such employee may be at stake for no fault of him.

Under any circumstances, no Manager should resort to the habit of back-biting which is injurious not only for him but also for the organisation and the employees too. Back-biting is considered as perversion of a person and no Manager with such habit can think of winning confidence in the higher management and working in any organization for a longer period of time. The employees working under him will heave a sigh of relief if such a Manager quits the organisation at the soonest.

The persons who have innate desire to work as Managers by acquiring required qualifications and also who are already working in managerial capacity, must not entertain any idea of becoming double standard persons with tendency of back-biting in the interest of their working as successful Managers. Persons practising the habit of back-biting are abominable and hypocritical. They cannot develop unblemished character. Such persons are unfit to shoulder higher responsibilities in the offices in the capacity of Manager, because they are derelict of managerial quality with such inclination of back-biting.

15

ATTITUDE

Positive attitude of a Manager contributes to success. It applies to every sphere of life including one's personal and professional life. A Manager cannot be a successful Manager without having positive attitude. Foundation of success depends upon positive attitude. A person with positive attitude is like a fruit of all seasons. The following are the benefits of positive attitude:

(a) Fosters team work in an organisation,

(b) Improves quality of work,

(c) Fosters better relationships with the higher Management, employees and the customers,

(d) Makes for congenial atmosphere,

(e) Generates loyalty in the minds of the employees,

(f) Helps solve problems.

Therefore, a Manager with positive attitude can have the advantage of all the above which will lead to his success in the field of his profession.

In this connexion, it will be appropriate to mention as to how to develop positive attitude, if a Manager is devoid of the same. The ways are:

(a) Be aware of the principles that build a positive attitude,

(b) Desire to be positive,

(c) Cultivate discipline and dedication.

The Managers should always bear in mind that negative attitude breeds bitterness and resentment in the minds of the higher management and the employees. Also a Manager with negative attitude is in the habit of finding faults with every employee and every situation which will negate systematic working in the office. Therefore, a Manager must abjure negative attitude in the interest of attaining success in the field of his profession.

16

What should be the Relation a Manager has to Maintain with the Subordinate Staff Members

Employees are no doubt inseparable members in an organisation. Although a Manager is one of the pillars of an organisation, the employees are the supporting pillars. Hence, the employees are to be given due weightage and cognisance of performance of their duties. It is not possible on the part of a Manager himself to do the entire job alone of his subordinates, although he is in the know of the job performed by them. A Manager has to depend upon the employees in the discharge of duties. Therefore, in order to run a company smoothly and efficiently, there must be complete cohesion and cooperation among the Manager and the subordinate staff members. Success of a Manager depends upon the cooperative attitude with the employees. Hence, in order to become a successful Manager, it is absolutely necessary that his relations and attitude with his subordinates will be:

(a) A Manager should treat the employees in such a way that they are not made to feel that they have no standing and status in the organisation. He should also create such a situation that the employees develop a sense of belonging to the company they serve and that they are always at the beck and call of the Manager.

(b) Human mind is very much touchy and sensitive. Therefore, a Manager should not injure the sentiment of the employees by talking with them in irrational way. By sweet words from the Manager, the minds of the employees are softened and work is performed in a vary peaceful atmosphere.

(c) A Manager has never to indulge in resorting to discriminatory attitude. He should treat all the employees with equal eyes irrespective of the position they hold. This will create homogeneity in the minds of the employees.

(d) He should have soft corner in his mind to understand the genuine difficulties of the employees and find his way to help the employees financially at times when they are badly in need of money arising out of their unforeseen and emergent financial commitments. This will help them to be worry-free and the work of the company will not meet with rebuff.

(e) Previously, the concept of employment was master and servant relations. But, now this concept has changed altogether as employee-employer relations. Therefore, although a Manager is a management staff, yet his relations with the subordinates will be very sweet and cordial in view of the changed situation in modern-day employment. This means that there should be close affinity between the Manager and the subordinate employees.

(f) Although close and sweet relations should persist between the Manager and the subordinate staff members, yet a Manager should not show laxity while dealing with the erring employees, else there will be slackening in the maintenance of administration, which will be disastrous for the organisation.

In order, therefore, to attain success and popularity, a Manager has to deal with the employees by the above principles, which is very important for all the Managers in the modern-day employment scenario.

17

INTELLIGENCE

Every Manager must have intelligence quotient (I.Q.). In his capacity as Manager since he may have to take many actions on the spot instantaneously he must be in the know that every action has reaction and in multiple cases such reactions may be detrimental to the interest of the organisation which he must avoid. But how? This will be possible when he has the intellectual capability and sharpness of mind to surmise what would likely to take place arising out of such actions taken by him. Here lies his success as a Manager. A Manager has obviously to deal with the intricacies of matters which require tactful handling in the interest of the organisation. Such tactful handling of matters requires his intelligence. A person without intelligence can never think of becoming a Manager, because he will be a bankrupt of managerial qualities in absence of the same.

Intelligence of a Manager helps overcome many problems which he faces during the course of his working. More so, by virtue of his intelligent decisions in matters of insurmountable problems facing any organisation, he paves the way to come in the limelight as a magnetic force in the eye of the higher management and his prospect in the organisation is widened. Needless to emphasise, intelligence is an indispensable qualification for a Manager. By virtue of his intelligence he will have quick grasping capacity of things which is one of the plus points to act as Manager. In order to work tactfully a Manager has to study the psychology and sentiments of the employees and this becomes possible when he has the analytical capacity and the intelligence of the Manager plays a great role in this respect.

It is evident how intelligence of a Manager is important in the performance of his duties. Such a Manager with intelligence quotient can never become unsuccessful.

This chapter will be incomplete if it is not discussed how intelligence of a person could be developed. It is of course an admitted fact that intelligence of a person has its own originality. But still then it could be developed further by the following methods which are analysed seriatim:

(a) Desire of a person to come to a definite conclusion after analysing the facts and circumstances of matters.

(b) Mixing up with different strata of people to know about their views of variegated nature.

(c) Mixing up with the galaxy of intellectuals to know about their perception of things.

(d) By way of gleaning practical experience.

(e) Propensity to know the unknown.

(f) Contemplation on any matter seriously to know its bright/dark side.

If all these are practised there will be broadening of mental faculties thereby developing intelligence of a person.

18

KNOWLEDGE OF LABOUR MATTERS

A Manager working in administration ought to have knowledge of the principles of labour laws, although there may be Personnel Manager/Labour Officer in the Organisation, whose function is to deal exclusively with the labour matters. Question arises—for what purpose the Manager should have knowledge of labour matters. There is of course no compulsion that the Manager in administration shall have to undergo course of personnel management. Administration is a department which deals with the manpower as also HRD in an organisation leaving aside other issues of importance. Administration and the employees are inter-connected and inseparable. In absence of employees administration is practically meaningless. Welfare and problems of the employees are the look-out of administration. Trouble-free running of an organisation depends largely upon the complacence of the employees and this complacence is related to the worthy and competent administration of the Manager.

Trade Unionism is a right of the employees as stipulated in the Indian Constitution. Labour Union is formed in order to counteract the unscrupulous and mal-administration of an organisation. A Manager has, therefore, to decipher the sentiments of the employees as to why they have turned violent and ventilated their grievances compelling them to form union, which is happening in many of the organisations. Instances are plenty that many organisations are conspicuous by its absence of labour unions and the employees are working for longer hours in the best interest of the organisation without any resentment. This is due to good governance of the organisation which depends much upon the way of administering the affairs by the Manager.

A Manager should bear in mind always that trouble-free running of the organisation lies mostly with the style of working of the Manager and not with the Personnel Manager/ Labour Officer, because policy matters concerning the employees of the organisation are dealt with by the administration and the Personnel Manager/Labour Officer has to extend his hand of cooperation with expert advice to the administration in the matter.

An Administrative Manager has to get himself conversant at least with the following as far as labour matters are concerned for the purpose of maintaining administration:

(a) Provisions of Industrial Disputes Act with subsequent amendments,

(b) Trade Union Act,

(c) Procedure for retrenchment/ lay-off of the employees,

(d) Procedure for holding domestic enquiry against the charge-sheeted employee, if the charges levelled against him are grievous,

(e) Formalities to be observed with the Labour Directorate in dealing with labour matters,

(f) Issuance of appointment letters to the employees in such a way that there may not be incorporation of any clause therein which will go against the interest of the organisation in case when dispute may arise with regard to employment.

These are the fundamental principles of labour matters a Manager has to know. Apart from the above, the Manager has to get himself conversant with other labour matters by discussions with the Personnel Manager/Labour Officer time to time. A Manager being in administration has also to take part in the bipartite/tripartite discussions with the leaders of Labour Union separately or combinedly with the Labour Directorate, so that he can also express his views in the matter of settlement of disputes.

It is, therefore, amply clarified that a successful Manager in administration has to get himself involved invariably with labour matters for the purpose of maintaining viability in his administration although there is Personnel Manager/Labour Officer in the organisation.

19

Keeping Healthy Mind and Sound Health

The duties of a Manager is as such that he has to deal with matters of importance and intricacies with cool brain and mind. A Manager possessing sound health is a person of activity, which is needed most to execute work with efficiency. Ill health devours his working capacity. Unless a Manager is a person of activity he cannot do justice to the work entrusted to him. He has not only to do office work but also to keep himself preoccupied with outside work such as contacting with the officials—both government and non-government—for getting jobs done successfully. For this purpose he is to be invigorated and activated with healthy mind and sound health.

Efficiency of a Manager could be maintained when he would keep himself busy in doing jobs entrusted to him by taking care of maintaining sound health and keeping healthy mind. On the other hand, he will prove himself inefficient when he will be falling sick sporadically and will continue to remain absent from attending office time and again which will affect his working very much. Therefore, in order to keep healthy mind with sound health, it is absolutely necessary that he has to go for excursion tours, duly arranged by the company at least once in every year. This will freshen his mind and body and he will feel enthusiasm to work with strength, vigour, zeal and freshness after return from such tours. The purpose of arranging such tours is to revitalise the working spirit of the Manager which will be of great advantage for the company too.

Apart from this, Managers are to be made members of Lions Club or any other clubs which are the concentration of galaxy of intellectuals. Mingling with the personalities attending to such clubs after office hours will be very much conducive for the Managers to lessen their clumsiness and fatigue after working in the office with tension. Mental make-up of the Managers will also be developed by mixing up with such personalities in the club and also it will help develop the business relations with different organisations which in turn will benefit the organisation in many ways. Becoming members of such clubs is, therefore, absolutely necessary for the persons working in managerial capacity to preserve their efficiency of working by way of keeping healthy mind and sound health and also for upkeep of business relations. This is also one of the factors as to how a Manager could be successful in the discharge of his duties and he will feel oneness to the organisation, which the higher management expect of a Manager.

20

Contributing Factors which Determine the Effectiveness of a Manager

When a Manager wants to be successful in his duties and functions doing justice to the organisation in his capacity as Manager, there must be contributing factors which would make him effective. An effective Manager is an asset of the organisation and is inalienable from the higher management. Such an effective Manager can enjoy the full confidence of the highest echelon of the Management. Here lies his greatest satisfaction and the co-officers and the employees will hold him in high esteem. The following are the contributing factors which determine the effectiveness of a Manager:

(a) Business Protocol

A Manager must have the sense of business protocol. Business protocol generates relationship, drives cooperation and fuels communication.

(b) Effective Listening

Effective listening by a Manager pleases employees and other people. This demonstrates his open mind, which is the key to communication. The essentials of effective listening are to list:

* Without interruption
* Without switching of
* With intent for understanding
* Avoiding distractions
* Showing respect and understanding
* Having eye contact with employees.

(c) Attitude

It is a way a Manager has to communicate his mood to others. Positive attitude is a mindset without which nothing worthwhile can be achieved. Positive attitude breeds positive results.

(d) Motivation

An effective Manager should encourage and inspire people to motivate themselves.

(e) Decision Making

An effective Manager has to identify the real causes of any problem before arriving at a decision. He has also to think of far-reaching consequences before arriving at a final decision.

(f) Relationship

An effective Manager must take special care to maintain relationship with the co-officers and the subordinates. In dealing with the subordinates, the important steps to be taken by the effective Manager are:

* Knowing the subordinates
* Lending ears to listen
* Showing patience
* Remaining firm but not angry.

21

STYLE OF FUNCTIONING OF A MANAGER

Style of functioning of a Manager plays a very important role to consolidate his position in the organisation where he works. He should work in such a manner that it does not irk the employees thereby generating discontent in their minds out of the discourteous way of his working. Keeping the employees happy by his style of working should be the motto of a Manager. A Manager will be alienated from the employees when his style of working is not to the liking of the employees. In such case he will be a misfit in the organisation. His working in the capacity of Manager will meet with rebuff and he will be the most unpopular Manager for his peculiar and strange way of working. Under the circumstances, is it worthwhile on the part of a Manager to pervert his normal style of working? The answer must be in the negative. Style of working of a Manager must be methodical befitting to the organisational set-up. A Manager will work with honour and dignity in the organisation only when his style of working will be on the following basis:

(a) A Manager has to keep the General Manager/President/Managing Director/Chairman of the Company abreast of the functioning of his section/department at regular intervals.

(b) Taking note of the points which the General Manager/President/Managing Director/Chairman directs for implementation and informing him/them of the progress achieved in this direction.

(c) Arranging meetings with the Section In-charges time to time to know about their problems, if any, for redressal.

(d) To give suggestions in writing for efficient running of the organisation to the General Manager/President with copy to Managing Director/Chairman.

(e) To obtain progress report of the working of the employees every fortnight from the Section Incharges.

(f) To maintain good liaison with the outsiders coming to the Company for business.

(g) To think of the development/progress of the organisation bearing in mind that it is his own organisation.

(h) To deal with the matters in the best interest of the organisation depending upon the exigency of circumstances.

(i) To take rational view in dealing with the employees.

(j) Finally, his style of working will be in conformity with the system of working prevailing in the organisation.

When the Manager will be able to mould his style of working in the above fashions he will be regarded as the most successful Manager of the organisation and will be considered an asset in the eye of the higher management.

22

A Manager as an Administrator

Competence of a Manager is adjudged by his way of administering the affairs in the best interest of the organisation. A Manager who is vacillant in his actions stumbles in his working at every step and in such case he is an utter failure to discharge his responsibilities. What is needed is that a Manager must be a person of strong will force and has controlling capacity. Employees will have the confidence in the actions taken by a Manager when the same are in the best interest of the organisation and the employees as a whole. A Manager must be a person having mental acumen and personality and then only he will be in a position to discharge his duties as an administrator in true sense of the term in the capacity of his designated post of Manager. His way of administration will be as such that he must be bold enough to deal with any knotty problems during the course of his working. His administration must be acclaimed with commendation in the eye of others. He must have the capacity to sort out even the invincible problems by applying his intellectual capability.

For the purpose of maintaining his administration in the best interest of the organisation, he must have argus eyes over what is happening all around his office so that his' administration does not end in fiasco. Higher Management has inviolable faith in the administration of the Manager when he justifies his capability by his foresightedness and experience. Maintenance of administration is vital for a Manager on which depends trouble-free running of the organisation. Hence, the Manager's responsibility in his performance as an administrator is a stupendous task.

It is an admitted fact that administrative acumen is wanting in many organisations. Capable Managers with administrative acumen are the panacea for the organisations facing closure on account of being sick, so that such organisations are restored for economic resuscitation. Competent Managers working in organisations must be fully devoted so that they prove themselves assets by virtue of their administrative skill. Managers working in the organisations must be fully trained up so as to enable them to push the organisations to ascend to the position of all-round viability by dint of their administrative skill and competence.

23

Ensuring Discipline and Dress of a Manager

Instances are plenty that many talented persons have not been crowned with success in their lives. They have not tried to realise that their failures to attain success were on account of their leading lives recklessly and in indisciplined way. Haphazard way of working is not discipline. Discipline is something different. Discipline is a regulated and systematic way of doing things. Peace and happiness of a person comes when he is disciplined. Practice of discipline helps a person reach the desired goal. Discipline is the yardstick for progress of human beings. Human life is now very much complex and hence easy and peaceful life is conspicuous by its absence in most of the cases. Disciplined way of working is the only answer to bringing peace, happiness and regulated life. Hence, discipline is very important for every human life.

Having discussed the importance of discipline in the foregoing, it is absolutely necessary that a Manager is also required to be disciplined. Otherwise, system of his working will be in complete disarray. In order to become a successful Manager he has to enforce discipline. Strong administration in an organisation is the result of the enforcement of discipline. In absence of maintenance of discipline by a Manager, employees become obstinate, reckless and uncontrollable which is pernicious for the organisation. Also when discipline is impaired lawlessness prevails everywhere and the organisation crumbles into economic degeneration and ultimately it is threatened with closure. Maintenance of discipline brings prosperity to an organisation. Disciplined way of working is the answer to attaining efficiency by a Manager and when he is efficient it is his responsibility to see that discipline is upheld. With a view to attaining this, he himself should be a man of discipline and then only he can enforce discipline in the organisation.

Dress of a Manager

There should be pink of perfection in the dress a Manager puts on. Office decorum is very important. Wearing decent dress by a Manager is a part of maintaining office decorum. Office of the Manager is prestigious and hence in order to maintain the prestige of his office, he should also put on decent dress. More so, by wearing dress of good taste a Manager looks a person of personality which speaks well of him in the eye of the higher management. Smartness of a Manager is an important factor for his efficient working and he looks smart when he wears good dress. Wearing quality dress he can also leave a good impression in the minds of the high officials of other organisations when he calls on them for any official purpose. So, wearing graceful dress by a Manager has tremendous impact in the business organisation.

24

Expressing Words of Appreciation

It is the psychological tendency of the employees that whenever they are rewarded with the words of appreciation from the Manager for the jobs performed by them to the atonement of the Management, they are enkindled with enthusiasm and inspiration and that they are devoted and inclined to do more jobs in better ways. Expression of words of appreciation by the Manager is thus a motivation for the employees. In this connexion, it is worthwhile to mention the saying of the psychologist, William James that—"One of the deepest desires of human beings is the desire to be appreciated."

For the good jobs done by the employees, the Manager has to express his feelings of appreciation in the following manner:

(a) The way the job has been handled by you is superb and commendable. Please continue to make efforts that the jobs to be done by you in future should also be performed in like manner.

(b) The expression of appreciation from the Manager must be sincere and from the core of heart and not from mouth. It should also not be a flattery.

(c) While expressing the words of appreciation the word, 'but' should not be used, as in the case of the sentence—"I do appreciate your handling the job in most efficient manner but..." *i.e.*, to be more precise the word 'but' is not to be used. Otherwise, it will be an appreciation with condition.

(d) The Manager should bear in mind that expressing the words of appreciation does not mean that he has to get the compliment from the employees in return *i.e.*, "Thank you, sir for your appreciating me."

This is all about the words of appreciation in the case of the jobs done by the employees successfully for the purpose of rejuvenating their spirit.

Managers know it well that "To err is human." Hence, it is not expected of the employees that they will be able to do flawless job all the times. In such case, the Manager should inspire them and appreciate their attempts, although they have not been successful in doing the job. The Manager should say, "Failure is the pillar of success and you should not get dejected." By such exhortation from the Manager the employees will not be down-hearted and that they will be earnest in their future course of working.

It is expedient that the Managers should not throw cold water upon the employees for their failure to do the job on any occasion but exhort and appreciate their attempt. Expressing words of appreciation to the employees is a part of duty on the part of a successful Manager, because he has to work with the employees whose collective endeavour is essential in the interest of the organisation.

25

How a Manager has to Maintain Good Relations with the Higher Management *vis-a-vis* Execution of Policy Matters

Trustworthiness of a Manager in the eye of the higher Management depends upon his honesty, integrity and sincerity and this ensures establishment of cordial relations between the higher management and the Manager. It is incumbent on the part of a Manager to know what are the factors which build trust. They are:

(a) A Manager should have openness of mind,

(b) He should have ability and attitude to serve,

(c) He should be a person of good character,

(d) He must have integrity which is the ingredient to trust,

(e) He must have consistency in his deeds and words,

(f) He should have politeness,

(g) He has to give due respect which shows his caring attitude.

It will be in the fitness of things if a Manager is in the know what are the factors which hinder maintenance of good relationship with the higher Management. They are:

(a) Lack of courtesy,

(b) Arrogance in attitude,

(c) Inconsistent behaviour,

(d) Lack of discipline,

(e) Negative attitude,

(f) Uncaring attitude,

(g) Lack of integrity,

(h) Voracious appetite for money.

When a Manager will be in the know that the above factors are standing in the way of building trust with the higher management, he has not to indulge in resorting to such acts in his own interest. There are people whom we love but we do not trust. So, trustworthiness is a greater compliment than love.

This is all about the explanation as to how a Manager has to create trust and good relationship with the higher management. Now, the following are the analyses as to how a Manager has to deal with the higher management for execution of policy matters, duly framed by them.

A Manager has to work under the suzerainty of higher management. Maintenance of interaction with them is an absolute necessity for a Manager to work in an organisation. He has to execute the policies of the higher management without contradiction. A Manager has to hold parleys with them at regular intervals and give nod to the policies framed by them without arguments and disagreements. He may, however, put forward his own opinion if he has to say anything in the matter and that too with civility and humility, so that there may not be any rupture and/or misunderstanding in the relations between the higher management and the Manager. Otherwise, the Manager will not feel plain sailing in the discharge of his duties and that his mind will be tormented always which may affect his continuance in the organisation. It is of course the entire responsibility of the Manager to work in the best interest of the organisation and hence any wrongs in the policies of the higher management, if there be any, should be mentioned with humility by the Manager, so that the higher management gives a second thought to the policies framed by them. This way of putting forward his opinion will deepen relations between the higher management and the Manager and he will gain confidence of the higher management thus paving the way for his future prosperity. A Manager has to ensure that he must not argue with the higher management on any matter under any circumstances and on any occasion.

26

Hard Work

Nothing is impracticable without strenuous labour. A man is crowned with success in his every effort when he puts in hard labour. Man rises to prominence and high position by dint of his vigorous work. Industry is the mother of success. Today is the age of cut-throat competition and survival of the fittest. There is no substitute for hard work. Idling away time brings misery and misfortune. Prosperity and self-development of a person are achieved through hard work only. In service career also employees ascend to high position by strenuous labour.

One cannot develop a capacity to do anything without hard work. "The harder you work, the luckier you get"—says Henry Ford. Success of a person does not come by accident. Everything that we enjoy is the result of hard work. Hard work makes a person better at whatever he is doing. Great talent without will-power and hard work is a waste. There is no magic wand for success. Excellence is not luck; it is the result of a lot of hard work and practice.

It is now crystal clear that when hard work is the panacea for attaining success, a Manager who is saddled with responsible and trustworthy jobs cannot resort to easy going habits and show laxity in the discharge of his duties. Otherwise, he will be a complete failure as a Manager. Success of a Manager as analysed above depends upon strenuous labour and he will enjoy the laurels of his exalted position. A hard working Manager is a very happy person and feels relieved of his duties, because of his hard work he can always keep the work up to date. Accumulation of work is caused by his easy going habits for which he feels mentally disturbed and he cannot do justice to the organisation through his work as Manager.

By virtue of hard work a Manager can excel in any obstacles which he may face during the course of his working and he will be crowned with success as Manager. A Manager can make things look easy when he has mastered the fundamentals of hard work. When a Manager is accustomed with hard work he forgets what is idle time and leisure time. The harder a Manager works, the better he feels; and the better he feels, the harder he works. In the real world, success comes to doers, not to observers.

Hence, the success of a Manager depends upon how much time he puts in doing hard work.

27

How to Think of Attaining Economy by Avoiding Wasteful Expenditures

A Manager who is an integral part of an organisation and on whose working the higher Management has complete trust and confidence, has to see how to attain all-round economy by avoiding wasteful expenditures. This is absolutely necessary for efficient running of the organisation. When the margin of profit of the organisation is pretty high resulting in slashing down of the overall expenses the organisation can only march forward to rapid development by way of diversification. This is possible when the Manager takes interest in avoiding wasteful expenditures of the organisation.

There are number of ways as to how wasteful expenditures could be avoided for which the Manager has to see that:

(a) Attachment of Company's cars should be limited to certain executives/officials in consideration of their importance and usefulness to the organisation. Maintenance of log book is a must in order to gauge the personal use of the cars beyond office hours. This will reduce expenses on cars.

(b) Expenses for outside trips on Company's business should be strictly as per the prescribed rules of the Company.

(c) Too much of fringe benefits allowed to the employees must be marginalised.

(d) There should be proper manning for working in every department according to which appointments of employees are to be made so that application of VRS is not felt a necessity subsequently entailing payment of substantial amount which will have extra burden on the Company.

(e) Salary/wage structure should be worked out depending upon the size and profitability of the organisation.

(f) For the employees other than those covered under E.S.I., the Company should go for mediclaim for certain amount in respect of the individual employees depending upon the quantum of their monthly salaries. This will exonerate the Company to make bulk payment of medical expenses to the employees who may be hospitalised for serious ailments.

(g) The Manager has to see that payment of donation is restricted to bare minimum.

(h) While it is the practice of the union leaders to submit to the Management capricious and unreasonable charter of demands, it is the responsibility of the Manager to bargain tactfully with them to come to terms reasonably in the matter of fixation of revised salary/wage structure and other financial implications so that the financial burden on the company is lessened in respect of making payment of Provident Fund contributions, increased amount of bonus, gratuity, leave travel concession, retirement benefits etc.

(i) Personal use of telephone in the office by the employees should be restricted.

(j) There should be rational use of electricity. In this connexion, there should be standing instruction that whenever any officer leaves his chamber, electricity should be put off.

(k) Double increments to the employees in special cases should be given on pragmatic basis, for which the recommendations of the departmental heads should be given due consideration.

(l) Unnecessary paper work should be avoided as also correspondence so as to reduce postage expenses which is now very high.

The above are the important heads which could be tapped for the purpose of possible reduction of expenses thereby ensuring the organisation to run economically and the Manager has to find his ways to implement the same and here lies his success and competence for the position he clings.

28

SELF-ESTEEM

A Manager must be a person of self-esteem. Self-esteem is defined as the way a Manager knows himself thoroughly. An ambitious Manager with high self-esteem will accept jobs with entire responsibility. A successful Manager has the following distinguishing features:

(a) He has positive attitude,

(b) He has sense of responsibility,

(c) He has conviction,

(d) He makes the employees ambitious and motivated,

(e) He has confidence,

(f) He has self-interest,

(g) He has understanding,

(h) He is disciplined,

(i) He has sensitivity,

(j) He has modesty.

Possession of all the above traits by a Manager is the result of his being a person of self-esteem. Self-esteem is, therefore, very important for a Manager. For his self-esteem he also gets respects from all and sundry for which he gets impetus to work with intense ardour and efficiency.

Following are the behavioural patterns of a Manager who has no self-esteem:

(a) He is a man of peculiar nature,

(b) He is self-centered,

(c) He is not willing to accept responsibility,

(d) He suffers from egoism,

(e) He is in the habit of making excuses of his own failures,

(f) His behaviour becomes erratic,

(g) He avoids to mix up with people.

Therefore, a Manager without self-esteem is a misfit in the office and hence he cannot be a successful Manager in the discharge of his duties—nay he is not at all worthy to cling to Managerial position without having self-esteem.

From what has been discussed in the foregoing, self-esteem is one of the essential ingredients of a Manager who wants to be successful in the discharge of his duties.

29

PRINCIPLES AND CHARACTERISTICS OF A SUCCESSFUL MANAGER

A successful Manager must have the following principles and characteristics:

Uprightness

A Manager must possess moral integrity. On no occasion he should be hypocritical. His actions and deeds must be straightforward. He must be honest to himself. He should keep himself engaged in constructive activities with positive attitude and straightforwardness.

Mingling with the People of Good Quality

A Manager has to form an association of persons with high moral character and virtuous quality. By mingling with such people his mental make-up will be moulded in such fashion that he will be a person of exaltation, which is absolutely desirable befitting to his managerial position. George Washington has said, "Associate yourself with people of good quality if you esteem your reputation, for it is better to be alone than to be in bad company."

Discipline

A Manager is obviously in the know that many problems are brought about by indiscipline. He should, therefore, be disciplined so that problems do not emanate so as to enable him to be free from problems as far as possible. A disciplined Manager is also an instance for other employees in the organisation, who are inspired to follow suit.

Patience

A Manager is saddled with load of work. If he becomes ruffled to handle the spate of work he is an utter failure to work in managerial position. A Manager must be undaunted and accept things easy. In such case, patience of a Manager plays an important role. With patience he can overcome any insurmountable problem and remain free from scares and anxieties. Patience is a virtue.

Abatement from Criticism

A Manager indulging in criticising others cannot be considered a respectable person. Habit of criticism speaks of the parochial mindedness of a Manager. He cannot draw respect from his subordinates. As a Manager when respectability is lost everything is lost which is hard to regain. A Manager is a distinguished person. If he is in the habit of criticising others he cannot be treated in high esteem and it is meaningless for such a person to work in managerial position. A Manager should, therefore, abstain from criticising others in the interest of upholding his position in the organisation. He will also draw respect from the higher management when he is not indulging in criticising others.

Quality of Forgiveness

Forgiveness is a great quality of a Manager. By his such quality he can keep the employees under his fold. No man is perfect. He has to commit mistakes because to err is human. It does not speak well that the Manager should go on censuring the employees always for the wrongs committed, rather he should educate them by showing the ways as to how commission of wrongs is to be annulled. When a Manager forgives the erring employees it displays highness of his mind. A successful Manager should, therefore, infuse in himself the quality of forgiveness.

Remaining Jovial

A Manager has to remain jovial and humorous. This will keep his mind light and free from anxieties which will help him to accomplish even the intricate work with ease and comfort. Success of a Manager depends upon his competence in performing work in apple-pie order when his mind remains undisturbed. His undisturbed mind is the result of his remaining joyous.

Endurance

Endurance is one of the qualities of a Manager. He must be steady and firm under any odds and ends. Lack of steadfastness as well as firmness is a weakness on the part of a Manager. A successful Manager should have endurance to do justice to his work.

Amiable Disposition

A person of amiable disposition is endeared by all. Amiable disposition of a Manager helps immensely to attain success in the discharge of his duties as he gets unstinted cooperation from all for his amiable disposition.

Manager—a Friend Outside Office Hours

Etiquette maintained in the office is something different. A Manager has to maintain his position in office for the sake of upholding discipline. If discipline is impaired for laxity of the Manager, chaos and confusion will reign supreme in the organisation. But, a Manager can mingle with the employees outside the office hours like friend of theirs. This will create affinity and freeness by the employees towards the Manager and also help them develop sense of belonging to the organisation.

Grooming up the Employees Working under Him

A successful Manager has to see that by his expert guidance the employees working under him are groomed up, which will help them consolidate their position and also enthuse them to learn new things of working paving the way for their elevation in future. Employees learn from their superiors and, therefore, a Manager has great role to play in moulding their future career.

30

CONCLUSION

A Manager attaining success in his working has also to take care of the following:

(A) RAPPROCHEMENT WITH OTHER OFFICERS OF THE COMPANY

It is very important that a Manager has to build confederation in maintaining cordial relations with other officers of the company. Even a powerful Manager will feel fish out of water if he has sordid relations with other officers of the Company. A Manager gets cooperation when he has built up cosy and sweet relations with other officers. Unity is strength which has to be preserved. There is a saying, "To have friends, be a friend." A Manager maintaining cordial relations with other officers will also be in the good books of the higher management. A Manager has to bear in mind the following ingredients to establish cordial relations with other officers of the company:

(a) He should maintain courtesy,

(b) His behaviour should not be inordinate,

(c) He should not have self-centeredness,

(d) He should have cooperative attitude,

(e) He should have amiable disposition,

(f) He should give due respect to other officers,

(g) He should not have negative attitude,

(h) His nature should not be suspicious,

(i) He should have a sense of compassion.

The above are the principal factors upon which positive relationship with other officers of the company is built.

(B) CLEAN AND PEACEFUL ATMOSPHERE

A Manager has to ensure clean and peaceful atmosphere in the office. This will entice the employees falling in love with office which in effect will improve their attendance. This will also generate enthusiasm in the minds of the employees to work with efficiency and zeal. A Manager should not unnecessarily inject tension in the minds of the employees. The employees should be kept peaceful always. If their mind is disturbed work will suffer. This should be another stratagem of a Manager as to how the employees should think of work only in such clean and peaceful atmosphere in their own interest.

(C) HAVING SOME IDEAS OF WORKING OF OTHER DEPARTMENTS

Although an Administrative Manager has not to interfere in the working of other departments, yet he should have some knowledge of their working, especially of Accounts, because working of this department is directly or indirectly connected with administration. When financial viability is there in an organisation, upholding of sound and strong administration will be made possible and the credibility of the Manager managing the affairs will be augmented.

(D) KEEPING ABREAST OF CURRENT AFFAIRS THROUGH READING OF NEWSPAPER DAILY

Newspaper is an encyclopaedia through which a person can glean all sorts of up to date knowledge. A Manager ought to be a person of knowledge which a newspaper can provide to him. In the business column of the newspaper many information relating to company affairs is ventilated and a Manager is required to be kept abreast of the same. This will enable him to communicate such information to the higher management which may be of interest to them.

(E) MISREPRESENTATION OF TRUTHS AND EXAGGERATION OF FACTS

In the eye of the higher management a Manager is a trusted and reliable person on whom responsibilities and many confidential matters of the company are entrusted with.

Therefore, a Manager must not entertain hypocrisy and take such action which will go against the interest of the organisation. Otherwise, his position in the organisation will be shaky. Distortion, misrepresentation and exaggeration of facts are not to be entertained by him so that he can continue to enjoy the confidence of the higher management, which is hard to build. A Manager is to cherish the idea that the confidence he gains from the higher management is his asset.

Questions and Answers

The job of a Manager is such that he must have broad-based knowledge of his working, for which he must be aware of the important provisions/stipulations. Possession of such knowledge will be conducive for him to work successfully as a Manager. Otherwise, he will have no *locus standi* to work in such capacity and there is every likelihood that he will meet with failure in the discharge of his duties in the true sense of term. I have, therefore, thought it prolific to discuss some of the important provisions/stipulations through questions and answers, as follows, and the Managers must have to keep themselves abreast of the same in their own interest.

Q.1. After prohibition of Contract Labour system in an organisation, can the workmen legally claim to be employees on regular basis?

Ans. Contract Labour system in an organisation can be prohibited by a Notification under the provision of the Contract Labour (Regulation and Abolition) Act, 1970. From the legal point of view, the workmen working under Contract Labour system cannot claim to be regular employees of the organisation, as they are not the employees of the organisation. If, however, the management of the organisation is desirous of appointing workmen for performing job on regular basis, they are to be given preference in such employment, if they are found suitable for the job.

In this connexion, it is of course pertinent to mention here that if the contract for supply of contract labour between the contractor and the organisation is deceptive, the workmen could be treated as employees of the organisation by regularising their services, in the event of abolition of Contract Labour system under the aforesaid provision.

Q.2. Is bonus an employee's right? When an organisation is losing, is it obligatory on the part of the owner to pay bonus? What is the difference between statutory bonus and bonus under a private agreement?

Ans. Under Section 1 of the Payment of Bonus Act, 1965, employees of every factory and any establishment employing 20 or more persons on any day in an accounting year, have statutory right to receive bonus, provided they worked for at least 30 working days in an accounting year. Section 36 of the Act empowers the Government to exempt an establishment from the provisions of the Act having regard to certain factors, e.g. financial position thereof. An employee has a right to receive bonus irrespective of the fact whether the employer is making profit or not particularly when the payment of bonus was initiated earlier in the organisation.

Statutory payment of bonus is made as per the Payment of Bonus Act, 1965. On the other hand, the employer and the employees may arrive at an agreement or settlement regarding payment of bonus payable to the employees in line with the provisions of the 1965 Act to determine the minimum quantum of bonus payable.

Q.3. If a Company declares closure of its undertaking, what is the consequence for the employees? What are the remedies open to the employees?

Ans. Section 2(cc) of the Industrial Disputes Act, 1947, defines "closure" as closing down of a place of employment or part thereof. The consequence for the employees is that their services are terminated. If it is a case of genuine closure, the employees are only entitled to notice and compensation as per Section 25-FFF of the 1947 Act. If the undertaking is closed down under unavoidable circumstances, the compensation shall not exceed an employee's three months average pay.

Unavoidable circumstances do not include factors like financial difficulties/losses of the employer.

If the closure is a strategem for a lockout under Section 2(1) of the Industrial Disputes Act, 1947 which means temporary suspension of work to counteract workmen's collective bargaining, the validity of the closure may be challenged before the Industrial Tribunal by the workmen concerned.

Q.4. At the time of leaving a Company an employee has not received his final settlement and in the meantime the Company has also changed its name. Under the circumstances, what is the way out to get his due payment from the Company?

Ans. If an employee had left the Company without transgressing the terms of employment and also he is legally entitled to get all his dues from the Company, for which they (Company) are dilly-dallying to clear his dues, the employee can always put his claim of getting the dues payable to him by the previous company by filing a civil suit. If the organisation is a government one, he can proceed under Article 226 of the Constitution against the employer. In the matter of getting payment of his dues, it does not matter that the Company has changed its name subsequently.

Q.5. What should be the recruitment policy for trainees in an organisation other than the trainees as per the Apprentices Act, 1961?

Ans. Trainees are appointed by an organisation not as per the Apprentices Act, 1961 but against permanent vacancies. Apprentices engaged (not appointed) for certain period are not the employees of the organisation, who are debarred from getting all other benefits of the organisation. These trainees/apprentices get some amount of allowance only from the organisation and not salary.

Trainees against regular vacancies are appointed either from the direct applicants or through advertisement in newspaper. For appointing the trainees the candidates are called for interviews after shortlisting the applications. Before appointing the trainees, their references are taken into account as also their medical tests are conducted to consider suitability of the candidates for the posts they are to be appointed. Generally, the trainees against permanent vacancies are appointed for a period of one year and after completion of traineeship the candidates are taken in regular employment fitting in grades as per the status of the employees. The trainees during their training period, unlike the trainees engaged as per the Apprentices Act, 1961, do not enjoy all the benefits similar to what the confirmed employees enjoy.

Q.6. Is it justified that a Company can issue termination letter to its employees giving three/one months' notice, as the case may be, as stipulated in the appointment letters, without assigning any reason thereof? In such case, can the employee fight it out?

Ans. As per Article 226 of the Constitution, an employee can of course challenge the arbitrary decision of the employer in termining his services without assigning any reason. This will be in the case of the employee working in public sector company, as such company cannot deal with its employees in arbitrary manner, although in the appointment letter it may be written clearly in one of the clauses that the services of the employee can be terminated after confirmation of his services by giving three/one months' notice or pay in lieu thereof without assigning any reason thereof.

In the case of working in a private limited Company, unless the employees are protected under the Industrial Disputes Act, it may not be possible to win success in filing case against the employer in the above situation. The basic reason is that the employee has accepted the terms of employment and the service rules of the Company by signing the duplicate copy of the appointment letter. The only consolation is that such a clause in the appointment letter is contrary to public policy and so it may go in favour of the employees other than working in managerial capacity.

Q.7. What is contractual service?

Ans. The job on which the employees are engaged for a certain period of years is a contract service. After completion of the contractual service it may not be renewed for a further period or in certain cases when the job necessitates continuity the contractual service may be renewed. Contractual service does not attract the retirement benefits like provident fund and gratuity as also other fringe benefits, as in the case of regular employment vis-a-vis the incremental salary. The person engaged on contractual service is not a regular employee of the company.

Q.8. In what way the terms of V.R.S. could be amended to make it more effective?

Ans. Voluntary Retirement Scheme (V.R.S.) is called the 'Exit Policy' or 'Golden handshake' or 'Separation Scheme'. It is of paramount necessity to make some changes in V.R.S. policy to get overwhelming response. When the number of educated youths are inflating in the country by leaps and bounds, who are aspiring for getting gainful employment, it will not be in the fitness of things to squeeze employment potentiality by the application of V.R.S. with no substitution by way of denying fresh appointment. Otherwise, it will have tremendous ill effects on the society. V.R.S. should not be made compulsory for all the employees in general, working in establishments. From the pragmatic point of view, V.R.S. should aim at retiring only the de-motivated and inefficient employees aged above 50 and replacing them with fresh hands. V.R.S. should also be made as an exit option to people who do not want to work any more. The objective of the scheme should not be to reduce man-power but improve its quality by infusing fresh blood without increasing its payroll cost to be able to match the new generation. This way of application of V.R.S. will weed out the unproductive and inefficient employees from the establishments and increase the efficiency in the working system with new blood who would be working side by side with the efficient employees even crossing 50 years of age.

Q.9. Will it be in order to put an employee on probation for a period of 12 months?

Ans. An employee who is put on probation on appointment is against permanent vacancy. On successful completion of probationary period, the employee is confirmed in his services. The purpose of putting the employee on probation is to gauge his working before confirmation.

As per labour law, an employee either he is appointed on training or on probation is eligible to claim permanency in his job after completion of 240 days of working and in this case he does not need to complete 12 months of training/probation. Therefore, it will be in the fitness of things if the training/probationary period is fixed initially for six months with provision for extension of the period by another three months.

As a good employer it is always better to stick to the labour laws in toto in all respects and any deviation from the same may lead to problems and complications.

Q.10. Will it be in order on the part of an employer to allow an employee to sign documents as authorised signatory without issuing any appointment letter to him?

Ans. An employee can of course sign many documents on behalf of the Company on instruction from the higher Management provided appointment letter has been issued to him. An employee in service on permanent cadre has to be issued appointment letter. Otherwise, his appointment in the organisation cannot be regularised as an employee on permanent cadre and in this case also he cannot sign documents on behalf of the company, because of absence of his *locus standi* as employee in the company.

Q.11. Can the services of a confirmed employee be terminated if he takes unathorised leave after expiry of sanctioned leave?

Ans. Absence from duty unauthorisedly by a confirmed employee after expiry of his sanctioned leave is no doubt a misconduct on his part, but on this ground his services cannot be terminated, as per the ruling given by the Allahabad High Court. The erring employee cannot be denied the right to explanation or an opportunity of hearing in the event of his being removed from services for taking unauthorised leave. Justice S.N. Srivastava of Allahabad High Court gave the ruling on a writ petition filed by M/s. DCM Limited, Ghaziabad.

Q.12. What is B.I.F.R.?

Ans. One of the most important legislations dealing with industrial sickness is SICA [Sick Industrial Companies (Special Provisions) Act, 1985] which provides for the establishment by the Central Government of a Board for Industrial and Financial Reconstruction (BIFR). BIFR consists of a Chairman and not less than two and not more than fourteen members.

When any Company becomes sick it is put on BIFR. After inquiry if BIFR is satisfied that the Company is unable to recoup the accumulated losses within a reasonable time, the Board feels expedient in the public interest to adopt certain measures for improving the performance of the Company and in such case it may direct any operating agency to prepare a scheme providing for such measures as expeditiously as possible but within a period of ninety days. After consideration of all the relevant facts and circumstances if the Company/industry is not likely to be viable in future, BIFR refers the matter to the High Court with its recommendation to wind up the sick industrial company in accordance with the provisions of the Companies Act, 1956.

Q.13. What is the difference between lay-off and retrenchment?

Ans. Lay-off as defined in Section 2(kkk) of the Industrial Disputes Act, 1947, broadly means the failure or inability of an employer to give employment to a workman whose name appears on the muster rolls of the industrial establishment, on account of shortage of coal, power or raw materials or accumulation of stocks or breakdown of machinery or natural calamity or any other connected reason. Lay-off is temporary and is different from retrenchment, as defined in Section 2 of the Industrial Disputes Act, 1947, which otherwise implies termination of service.

During the period of lay-off, the workman concerned are not required to work but are entitled to compensation as per the provisions of Section 25C of the Industrial Disputes Act. However, they may be retrenched in terms of Section 25F of the said Act after the first 45 days of lay-off.

An employer coming within the purview of the Industrial Disputes Act cannot resort to lay-off at its sweet will. It has to obtain prior permission of the appropriate government or such authority as the government may specify before laying-off a workman (other than a badly or casual workman).

Q.14. Is it in order to terminate an employee without assigning any reason during the period of probation?

Ans. The fact is that a probationer cannot claim to be a permanent employee till such time he is confirmed in his services, although a probationer is appointed against a permanent vacancy. If, however, the management has to dispense with the services of a probationary employee, it will be in the fitness of things and an act of genuine labour practice to issue him a letter asking him to be more particular in the discharge of his duties during the extended period of his probationary service by another three months or so, as stipulated in the letter of appointment. This means that he is to be given chance to improve upon his performance during probation and that the union leaders will also be satisfied that by such letter the management has given opportunity to the incumbent to improve upon his working before he is confirmed. Even if his performance is not found satisfactory during the extended period of probation, his services may be terminated. In this connexion, it is pertinent to mention here that in the letter asking the probationary employee to improve upon his performance, the Management has to mention specifically the shortcomings in the discharge of his duties, without which the letter in question will not stand.

Q.15. If a probationary employee is not issued letter confirming his services after completion of his probationary period/s, is it correct to assume that such employee is still on probation?

Ans. When the concerned employee has successfully completed his probationary period/s, he is automatically confirmed in his services from the next date of expiry of probationary period/s, even if letter confirming his services has not been issued by the Management. However, in order to make the service records file of the employee complete and up to date, it is necessary that such letter has to be issued at a later date also, if it was not issued immediately on completion of his probationary period/s.

Q.16. Can the services of a confirmed employee be terminated without assigning any reason?

Ans. Termination of services of a confirmed employee without any cause or reason and also without adhering to other formalities *i.e.*, holding of domestic enquiry, is wholly arbitrary and a breach of the principles of natural justice. If the service contract attracts the provisions of the Industrial Disputes Act, 1947, it will be an industrial dispute in terms of the said Act whereupon the Industrial Tribunal will adjudicate the same. Otherwise, the terminated employee may challenge the dismissal by way of a writ petition before the High Court.

Q.17. If an employee meets with an accident while on duty on Company's job and is not likely to resume duty within 15 days or more, will he get salary for the number of days of his absence on medical ground and also the reimbursement of the expenses incurred for such medical treatment?

Ans. One of the terms of appointment in the private organisation is that an employee is entitled to get full or half reimbursement of salary for a certain period of his absence on normal medical ground. But, if the terms of employment of the organisation is silent in providing payment of salary to the employee, in such case, the company would be bound to pay salary during the period of his absence on medical ground till recovery. This is for the specific reason that the employee had met with an accident during the period of his working on Company's job—whether at site or outside on travelling *i.e.*, on way to reporting to duties, or otherwise.

With regard to reimbursement of medical expenses, unless otherwise the employee is covered under any Act or is liable to be paid by other agency, the Company has also to reimburse medical expenses to such employee.

Q.18. Supposing, an employee has already completed 6/9 months probationary period/s as per the terms of appointment letter but no letter of confirmation was issued to him by the appointing authority after completion of probationary period/s. In such circumstances, can the employee tender resignation without giving one/three month's notice, as the case may be, which a confirmed employee is required to do after confirmation of his services?

Ans. It is an admitted fact that if an employee could complete the probationary period/s as per the terms of appointment letter, he is automatically confirmed in the post, although no letter of confirmation was issued to him by the appointing authority. But, in the absence of any letter of confirmation, an employee could surely tender resignation without giving any notice period for taking up employment elsewhere, for the very specific reason that non-issuance of letter of confirmation after successful completion of probationary period by the employee is the fault on the part of the appointing authority and in such case the Management has to accept the resignation without claiming any notice pay, although he is a confirmed employee without letter of confirmation. In fact, the employee has to get documentary evidence of his confirmation by way of a letter.

Q.19. In order to prove allegation and misconduct levelled against an employee it is the convention that domestic enquiry is held. If the misconduct is proved in the domestic enquiry without giving any opportunity to the delinquent and also without furnishing the copy of the proceedings of the domestic enquiry to the erring employee, is it correct to dismiss him?

Ans. The Enquiry Officer in his enquiry report never suggests punishment to the erring employee by way of dismissal, but mentions that the allegations and misconduct levelled against the employee have been proved. Dismissal of an employee is an extreme punishment taking into account the gravity of the misconduct committed. In the instant case, although the misconduct is proved in the domestic enquiry and if it is not a gross misconduct, the punishment warranted should not be dismissal.

In the domestic enquiry the delinquent has to be given all opportunity to defend his case by allowing him to engage his own expert in labour matters for examining and cross examining the management's witnesses. When it is not done, the maximum punishment of dismissal is also void.

Another important aspect is that after completion of the enquiry proceedings, copy of the enquiry report of the Enquiry Officer should also be given to the erring employee. If it is not done, it is an unfair labour practice. Under the circumstances, the employee is within his absolute right to challenge the decision of the Management to dismiss him, by way of writ petition in the High Court having jurisdiction in the matter. If the employee succeeds in the case, although the chance is extremely fair, he will be reinstated in his post with back wages.

Q.20. What is meant by sickness of a Unit?

Ans. In usual term a sick unit is that unit which is not healthy. In the eye of an investor it is the unit which has gone beyond the capacity of giving dividends. An industrialist opines that it is the unit which is suffering financial loss and is on the verge of closure. As per the Reserve Bank of India, an industrial unit is considered as sick when it has incurred financial loss for the past one year and it is likely to continue to incur the loss in the next two years also. This definition of the Reserve Bank of India is applicable for the registered Companies only which has been operating business for at least seven years.

Q.21. What are Holding and Subsidiary Companies and what is the difference between the two?

Ans. When a Company has control over another Company, it is known as a Holding Company and the Company so controlled by the Holding Company is called a subsidiary Company.

The analyses of the Subsidiary Company are as follows:

(i) When the composition of the Board of Directors of the Company is controlled by another Company, it is a Subsidiary Company.

(ii) When the majority of the shares of the Company is held by another Company, it is a Subsidiary Company.

Q.22. What is Memorandum and Articles of Association and what is the purpose of it?

Ans. For the purpose of floating a Company, the promoters of the same are required to draw up a Memorandum and Articles of Association, mentioning therein the name of the Company and determining the location of its registered office. This Memorandum and Articles of Association is to be submitted to the Registrar of Companies for the purpose of getting the Company registered with him. Once the Company is got registered, it becomes a legal entity. The Memorandum and Articles of Association is a very important document of the Company, because it contains the fundamental conditions upon which the Company is got incorporated. The Memorandum and Articles of Association is required to be drawn up in case of a Public Limited Company or a Private Limited Company.

Q.23. What is the difference between a Public Limited Company and a Private Limited Company?

Ans. A Public Limited Company is formed by a minimum of 7 (seven) subscribers and there is no maximum limit to the number of shareholders. A foreign national or a non-resident Indian can also be a shareholder subject to the approval of the Reserve Bank of India. Having wide membership by a Public Limited Company, a number of regulatory provisions are made under the Company law to exercise control over the working of such Company.

A Private Limited Company is formed by a minimum of two members with a maximum of 50 (fifty) members. Its shares cannot be transferred freely. Such a Company is also prohibited from inviting the public to subscribe to its shares or debentures. Private Limited Companies are, however, not subject to all the regulatory provisions which are applicable to Public Limited Companies.

Q.24. What is meant by 'Industrial Relations'?

Ans. The term, 'Industrial Relations' has no precise definition. However, the inner meaning of 'Industrial Relations' is the interaction between employer and employees, employees and employees, employers and employers and also between the state employers and employees. Industrial Relations are an integral aspect of social relations emanating from employee-employer interaction. The Industrial Relations deal with as to how the employees get on together at their work place, what difficulties are faced by them, how is the relation with the employer pertaining to salary/wages and working conditions and how the organisations are keen to protect the interests of the employees.

Q.25. What are the causes of industrial disputes?

Ans. There are a number of causes of industrial disputes. A dispute may be caused by any one or more of the following factors:

(a) Industrial dispute may be caused arising out of the demand of the employees/workmen for higher bonus on the ground that the organisation has been making substantial profits and the Management is depriving the employees/workmen from paying profit sharing bonus.

(b) Labourers generally want healthy and congenial working environment apart from good dealings from the management. But, if the management does not care for the human factor, conflict between the employer and the employees is bound to develop.

(c) When automation leads to retrenchment of employees, it is likely to cause a dispute.

(d) Demand for higher salary/wages is one of the most important factors of industrial dispute, when the employees feel that their salary/wages are not commensurate to their output of work.

(e) When the salary/wages are not sufficient to provide for a reasonable standard of living of the employees, conflict starts developing.

(f) When the salary/wages and other allowances are lower than those of the employees/workmen of other comparable enterprises, there is the dispute between the employers and the employees.

(g) When there is no job security of the employees/workmen in the enterprise arising out of the sporadic retrenchment/dismissals, the employees urge the management to protect job of the employees and dispute is caused in the event of paying scant attention by the Management in the matter of upholding job security.

(h) When there is no congenial working condition, such as length of working hours, interval and frequency of leisure, physical work environment, safety measures and the like, dispute is bound to arise.

(i) When the Management does not pay any heed to maintain labour welfare, such as canteen facilities in the establishment employing more than 250 workmen, rest and recreation facilities, accommodation facilities for the workmen staying at a distance from their houses, washing and bathing facilities, arrangement for drinking water, health services including occupational safety, arrangement for prevention of fatigue and any other matters of labour welfare, industrial dispute is caused.

(j) In the absence of effective personnel management, grievances and unrest which could be solved at the nascent stage, disputes also spark off.

These are the important factors which lead to industrial disputes.

Q.26. What are the ways and means to resolve the industrial disputes?

Ans. It is always desirable that industrial disputes are not allowed to surface in the interest of ensuring running of an establishment trouble-free, taking in view that prevention is better than cure. For this, the measures like good personal management, cordial employer-employee relationship, participation of labour in management, good employer-employee communication system, proper understanding of the situation by both the parties, mutual respect for each other's rights, proper discharge of the responsibilities by both the parties, etc. are very important to avoid industrial disputes.

There are statutory and non-statutory methods to settle industrial disputes. When the Management and the employees' representatives sit together across the table without third party interference for settling the disputes, it is termed as non-statutory method.

If the non-statutory method *i.e.*, the bipartite settlement of the industrial disputes becomes a failure, such disputes are referred to the conciliation officer of the concerned State Government for adjudication of the disputes. This is termed as statutory method of settling industrial disputes of an establishment.

Q.27. Can any employer deny granting of maternity leave to a married woman employee?

Ans. Entitlement of maternity leave by a married woman employee in the event of her pregnancy and after child birth covering three months with full pay is as per statute, as there is a legislation titled 'Maternity Benefit Act, 1961'. Many organisations may, however, be outside the purview of that statute but have their own policy for maternity benefits which includes granting of leave.

Such being the circumstances, whether the Company has maternity benefits as per the statute or not, it is obligatory to extend this benefit by the Company to the married woman. Any denial of granting the maternity benefit/leave will be in contravention of the terms of employment of the organisation.

Q.28. If the action taken by a Manager is not liked by the employees in general, what is the course left for him?

Ans. It is of utmost necessity that the Manager has to think twice before taking any action/decision, because he must be in the know that every action has reaction and this reaction may be detrimental to the interest of the employees. Taking of any action/decision hastily is never recommended and the Manager has to be meticulous in the matter. If the employees show resentment/consternation over such action of the Manager, it will of course not be in the fitness of things to rescind the decision, else it will speak ill of the competence of the Manager. For the purpose of upholding strong administration he cannot yield to the pressure of the employees who want to dictate terms over his action.

In order to avoid sordid atmosphere in the office over such issue tactful handling of the matter by the Manager is the immense necessity. But how? First of all, the Manager has to bring the employees into confidence. They should be impressed upon that such decision had to be taken by the Management at the instance of few of the nagging employees and, therefore, for the sake of upholding administration in the organisation taking of such action/decision was felt a necessity. But, in any case the interest of the employees who are sincere and loyal to the organisation will not be affected and the Management will take care of the same. The Manager has also to impress upon the employees that taking such action/decision time to time is necessary for upholding administration in the organisation, which is also common to all organisations. This way the consternation/agitation of the employees could be tamed by a successful Manager.

Q.29. If the employees are over burdened with work, will it increase their efficiency?

Ans. Every employee has certain capacity to bear load of work. Constant pressure with heavy load of work will surely decrease efficiency of the employees in the long run and that they will not be able to work with perfection. Employees are appointed to work and not for whiling away time for inadequacy of work. On account of lesser work the employees will be lethargic in consequence of which they will prove themselves inefficient. Therefore, it will not be in order if the employees are either over burdened with work or they are put with less work. In both the cases, the employees cannot attain efficiency. At times, due to exigency of circumstances the employees may be over burdened with work. But this will be a temporary phase. A Manager has, therefore, to see that the employees are distributed work in such a way that they can systematically complete their allotted work without accumulation.

It has been observed that in many cases, a Manager gives constant pressure of work to the employees who are efficient. This is not correct. For shouldering heavy load of work constantly, as allotted by the Manager, the employees will be rendered inefficient in due course of time.

Q.30. In what way the Managers are for 24 hours service in the organisations?

Ans. Managers are the pillars and magnates of organisations. Their services are unlike those of the general category of staff members who have fixed working hours in the office. The contributions of Managers lead to the efficient running of the organisations. In fact, in all respects they are part and parcel of the highest echelon of the Management and that they are always at their beck and call. Even after the working hours they are not to be inalienated from the working of the organisation. Many a times the Managers continue to talk with the higher management on phone from their residences on policy matters of the organisation. This indicates that even after their working in office they cannot shirk off their responsibilities. Managers are not workmen within the purview of Industrial Disputes Act. This is also another factor why they cannot cling to fixed working hours. Moreso, their functions are as such that they cannot wash their hands of the responsibilities they shoulder which require long hours of working. At emergent situation of the organisation, their presence is also called for even at the odd hours of the night. This way the Managers are for 24 hours service of the organisation.

Q.31. Contribution to the Provident Fund by the employees is a statute. When it is so, is it obligatory that the candidates appointed on regular basis after post retirement service should also contribute to provident fund?

Ans. Instances are plenty that candidates even after their superannuation from the same organisation or from other organisations are appointed on regular basis, if they are found quite hale and hearty and efficient. In such case, it is not obligatory that such employees should contribute to provident fund; because the superannuated employees after their fresh employment are not liable to be the members of provident fund and hence it is not a statute that they should contribute to provident fund.

In this connexion, it is to be noted that it will not be in order to appoint such hands in the regular service of the organisation but in contractual employment and in such position these hands will get allowance only without getting any other financial benefits and not salary, as salary is drawn by the employees who are on regular service only. Candidates engaged on contractual service are not treated as the employees of the organisation.

Q.32. Supposing, in the enquiry proceedings an employee has been exonerated from the charges levelled against him and accordingly he has been allowed to resume his duties and the management has paid all the dues to him which were withheld during the period of suspension. (During the period of suspension an employee is only to get subsistence allowance). After the employee resumed his duties he has not been allocated any work by the management and he has been kept idling away in the office for want of work. Now, the question is—can the management act like this?

Ans. When the charges framed against the employee could not be substantiated in the proceedings of domestic enquiry, it is the discretion of the management whether to allot work or not to the employee after he resumes duties and the employee concerned cannot compel the management to allot him work. Non-allotment of work to the employee is due to the fact that since the charges levelled against the employee have been nullified in the proceedings of domestic enquiry, it has become a rebuff to the management and it may be the strategem of the management to get rid of the employee as he is likely to relinquish his services with the company being humiliated for want of any work in the company.

Q.33. What is the justification that the Management should not send registered A/D letter to a delinquent employee at his house putting it in an envelope?

Ans. There is always the probability that a delinquent employee can deny receipt of letter addressed to him when it is put in a registered A/D envelope. The reason which he may adduce is that he has received only the envelope without any letter inside. Under the circumstances, the Management has again to deliver to him copy of the same letter when the delinquent employee reports on duty, which will not strengthen the case when the management wants to take any action against the employee. Any letter of charge-sheet has to be issued by the management maximum within two days of committing the offence by the employee. But, if receipt of such letter of charge-sheet is denied by the employee on account of the above reason, the management may be put in a bit embarrassing position. Management will, therefore, be in safe position if inland registered A/D letter is despatched to the delinquent employee and in that case the employee will not find any ground to deny receipt of such letter.

Q.34. Should a Manager consider appointing a candidate who was once working or is presently working with the competitor's organisation?

Ans. It will be in the fitness of things if a Manager avoids appointing a candidate who was once working or is presently working with the competitor's organisation. The reason is that such candidate must be owing allegiance and/or maintaining cordial and informal relations with his erstwhile or present organisation. Therefore, there is risk always that he is likely to pass on confidential information of the company to them if he is appointed and so such employee will be harmful for the organisation. Under the circumstances, it will be wise if such candidate is not considered for appointment even though he is found quite suitable for the post.

Q.35. It is very important for a Manager to maintain sweet employee-employer relations. What are the benefits out of it?

Ans. Sweet employee-employer relations benefit both the employees and the employers. Employees tend to have more inclination to work for the organisation treating it as their own which leads to efficiency in the running of the organisation. This inclination to work depends upon the recognition of the services of the employees by the management and satisfying them in the matter of fixation of proper salary and other fringe benefits so that the employees could work with free mind and without thinking of financial stringency. Efficiency in the working of the employees is achieved when they are satisfied having cordial employee-employer relations. By such efficient working of the employees the organisation naturally forges ahead of prosperity. Troubled organisation is a sign of degeneration which can be arrested by maintaining sweet relations with the employees. Therefore, sweet and cordial employee-employer relations are the essence of benefits for both the employees and the employers.

Q.36. It is important for a Manager to know what is ideal work environment.

Ans. Ideal work environment is very important to attain prosperity by any Company. Ideal work environment is defined as follows:

(a) Cleanliness in the office,

(b) Better working condition,

(c) Better salary to the employees which inspires them to work more,

(d) Right job for the right employees,

(e) Punctuality in attendance,

(f) Full devotion to work by the employees,

(g) No gossiping by the employees leaving the place of work,

(h) Pin-drop silence in the office,

(i) All officers and employees have to speak in decent way,

(j) Obedience to the superior officers.

Q.37. If any employee is not sincere to his duties and keeps the work in arrear what should be the course of action the Manager has to take?

Ans. Depending upon the extent of laxity of work done by the employees, the Manager should take action like:

(a) He should issue letter of warning. Even after receiving the letter of warning, the employee does not amend, his annual increment should be stopped by issuing a final letter asking him to be very particular in his working in future.

Or

(b) He should be made to understand by sweet words that his growth in the organisation is in his own hands and so he should work in the company with utmost sincerity in his own interest.

Or

(c) He should be transferred to other branch of the company as punishment. This course of action should be taken when the employee is beyond rectification.

Q.38. In what way a Manager of a company can increase the working efficiency of the employees?

Ans. (a) If any employee commits mistakes in his working, he should be advised in a mild way as to in what way the work could be done in a proper way.

(b) The Manager should exhort and encourage the employees to do work and should not show red eyes to them if they commit mistakes in their working.

(c) A Manager should be approachable always by the employees.

(d) The employees who are working with sincerity althrough should be rewarded by way of good increments/ex-gratia payment/promotion.

(e) A Manager should look to the personal difficulties of the employees and give them some financial assistance to tide over their problems.

(f) The employees should be made to feel that they are inseparable from the company and that they are not working merely for the sake of monthly salary only.

(g) During the course of working, a Manager should also discuss official matters with the employees—but not of course in all the cases. By such discussion the employees will feel more attached to their working.

If all these tactics are adopted by the Manager, efficiency in the working of the employees is bound to increase.

Q.39. If some of the employees/workers are not willing to do overtime as per the directive of the Manager what will be the course of action to be taken in the matter?

Ans. On account of break-down of machinery in the factory or for increasing the targeted production or for keeping the pending work up-to-date, the employees/workers are supposed to do overtime work on overtime payment which is a part of their duty, as recommended in the labour law. Therefore, the employees/workers cannot refuse to do over time work as per law, if it is within the permissible limit of overtime hours. Under such circumstances, the Manager within his right can ask the employees/workers to do overtime work. In spite of the fact, if the employees/workers are not willing to do overtime work, the Manager should issue show-cause notice to them before taking disciplinary action in the matter. But, the best course of action will be to talk to the Union leaders, if there is labour union in the organisation, so that good sense prevails upon the employees/workers not to refuse to do overtime work in future. It is not of course wise to incite the employees/workers by taking tough line of action on such issue for maintaining peace in the organisation.

Q.40. If an employee is very irregular in his attendance and remains absent from duty every now and then, what action is required to be taken by the Manager against such employee?

Ans. Irregular attendance as well as remaining absent from duty every now and then on the part of an employee is a misconduct. Such employee spoils the discipline of the organisation. There is also probability that other employees may follow suit. Under the circumstances, it necessitates to take disciplinary action against the erring employee. Such employee has to be warned in writing to improve upon his attendance if verbal advice fails to rectify him. Even if he does not amend his ways, his annual increment has to be stopped. But, in this case he has to be informed by a letter the reason of stoppage of his annual increment. Still then if he continues to act in the same way and is beyond rectification, pressure tactic is to be exerted on him, so that he starts feeling that his days are numbered in the organisation which will prompt him to seek service elsewhere.

If the employee continues to remain absent from duty without information and/or sanction of leave for more than seven days at a stretch, it is a gross misconduct on his part. If the employee has formed the habit of remaining absent from duties unauthorisedly he is liable to be dwelt with strongly as per law. For taking disciplinary action against him he is to be issued charge-sheet to explain his position and if the reply of the employee to the charge-sheet is not found satisfactory, domestic enquiry is to be held. If he is found guilty of the offence committed by him in the enquiry, appropriate punishment has to be inflicted upon him. It should be noted that dismissal from service is an extreme punishment which may be avoided by inflicting other exemplary punishment in such case. In this connexion, it is pertinent to mention here that commission of minor mistakes of similar nature thrice becomes a gross misconduct on the part of an employee.

It is advisable that the management should always remain on the safe side in dealing with the erring employees by sticking to the principles of labour laws, so that the union leaders do not find fault with the management in their action.

Q.41. What is Turnaround Management?

Ans. It is essential on the part of a competent Manager to know what is Turnaround Management. Turnaround Management refers to certain management measures which are taken by the higher management for the purpose of rejuvenating an organisation. The measures are:

(a) *Management Factor*

Managerial inefficiency is a very important reason

creating problems for an organisation. Therefore, it has been felt an imperative need to improve the quality of management. For this purpose, the higher management appoints an efficient Chief Executive Officer who has to streamline things and change the organisational culture.

(b) *Financial Management*

It is the inevitable part of Turnaround Management to arrange additional finance, setting of financial discipline as also financial restructuring.

(c) *Marketing Strategy*

Several organisations have to face many problems in absence of their marketing strategy. Evolving proper marketing strategy helps improve the position. Marketing strategy including the following:

(i) Entering into new markets,

(ii) Withdrawing from certain markets,

(iii) Developing markets and new customers.

(d) *Production Facilities*

Modernisation and improvement of plant and machinery are an important part of Turnaround Management. The measures are aimed at achieving uninterrupted production, better capacity utilisation, quality improvement, avoiding wastage and increase in productivity thereby reducing cost of production.

(e) *Human Resource Factor*

In respect of Turnaround Management human resource is also one of the important factors which includes the following:

(i) Surplus manpower should be done away with,

(ii) Morale of the employees should be boosted,

(iii) Quality of manpower should be improved through training and recruitment of competent people especially for key positions.

(f) *Miscellaneous Turnaround Management*

Miscellaneous Turnaround Management includes disposing of useless assets, closing down of some of the divisions/business, better management or procurement of raw materials and controlling emoluments of the employees.

The above are the ingredients of Turnaround Management which if properly implemented can ensure viability of any organisation.

Q.42. If an employee submits resignation either with immediate effect or with effect from a subsequent date, which has been accepted by the Management and if the employee withdraws it by a letter subsequently, should the management consider his letter of withdrawal of resignation?

Ans. After submitting letter of resignation by an employee, if it is accepted by the management, the request of the employee by a letter for withdrawal of his resignation may not be acceded to, because after accepting the resignation it is the discretion of the management whether to give due consideration of the letter of withdrawal of resignation of the employee or not. On the other hand, if the management has not accepted the resignation immediately and the employee has requested the management by a letter desiring to withdraw his resignation, the management will not find any ground to accept his resignation and in this case the original letter of resignation of the employee will be nullified.

Q.43. Can an employee submit resignation during the currency of availing of leave?

Ans. It is not proper on the part of an employee to submit resignation during the period of availing of leave. If any employee has in mind to submit resignation he has to report back on duty first after expiry of leave or after cutting short of his leave and then submit resignation. Management is not, therefore, bound to accept such resignation of an employee. The employee cannot go to the court of law for non-acceptance of resignation by the management in the instant case and non-settlement of his dues in the event of his resignation submitted during the period of his availing leave.

Q.44. How is the life of a Manager?

Ans. A Manager is a person of nimbleness. His life is blended with both solicitude and charm. In the office he is saddled with multitudinous work spiced with problems of variegated nature and the solution of the same lies with his tactful handling of the situation. His mental acumen helps a lot to arrive at a comfortable solution of such difficult and hard task. Most of the time his mind is obsessed with tension. But, still he has to remain calm and quite. Otherwise, he will look ruffled and agitated which will be damaging to his reputation as a Manager.

On the other hand, he feels exalted in the discharge of his duties being crowned with such position. He enjoys credibility when things are solved to the advantage of the organisation and feels inalienable from the higher management thus solidifying his position in the organisation and in such case he derives respect as a worthy and competent Manager. Remaining in such exalted position a Manager gets opportunity to mingle with the galaxy of intellectuals which helps broaden his mind. For his working in such position he also gets esteem in the society he lives. Since a Manager is a person of responsibility there is every reason for his vaunting that he is a worthy citizen of the country. He has to freshen his mind always for passing through tribulations.

Q.45. What should be the criteria the Managers should consider for appointment of candidates in different positions of ministerial rank and beyond?

Ans. Quality employees are the assets of an organisation of repute which runs with utmost efficiency with the galaxy of such employees. It is a known fact that the candidates who are recommended for employment are not generally of considerable worth and such candidates are to be nullified for employment as far as possible barring aside of course in the case of such candidates who are apparently found suitable after overall consideration. The following criteria are to be taken into consideration while appointing candidates:

(a) The Manager who is an interviewer should study the candidates' character, intelligence, smartness, temperament, alertness, presence of mind, patience, gentleness, way of thinking, personality and family background.

(b) Consistent academic career is to be taken note of.

(c) It is to be observed about the candidates' capacity of proper expression of things and whether they are well behaved.

(d) Candidates are to be considered for employment possessing sound health.

(e) Whether the candidates are dynamic and have foresightedness.

(f) Whether the candidates have sense of cleanliness and good habits.

(g) Candidates who are in the habit of irrelevant and unwanted talks should not be considered for appointment.

(h) Whether the candidates have aptitude. Attitude of the candidates has also to be closely studied.

(i) The candidates must have general awareness.

Apart from the above, the following are also to be taken into account for the purpose of finding suitability of the candidates:

(i) Intelligence

(ii) Self-confidence

(iii) Overal appearance

(iv) Behavioural pattern

(v) Ability to convince

(vi) Clarity of expression

While it may not be expected of the candidates appearing at the interviews for ministerial positions to fulfil all the above, the candidates for important positions should satisfy the interviewers in respect of their competence fulfilling all the afore-said criteria for suitability of their candidature.

Q.46. What are the criteria to give promotion in service to the employees in higher positions?

Ans. In the government organisations the criteria for promotion of employees are seniority in service and also qualifying in the departmental examinations. But, it is not so in case of private organisations where the criteria for promotion of employees to higher positions are:

(a) Capability of doing work with utmost efficiency,
(b) Development of mental faculty,
(c) Leadership quality,
(d) Length of service,
(e) Way of expression of things,
(f) Relationship with other employees and officers,
(g) Conception of ideas,
(h) Grasping power.

Q.47. What are the functions of a Manager in general?

Ans. While a Manager has multifarious duties to perform, both inside and outside the office in view of his position, the functions of a successful Manager in general are listed below:

(a) Streamlining the work of the organisation whenever it is not done in proper manner,
(b) Proper functioning of administration has got direct bearing with finance. A Manager has, therefore, to see the financial aspect directly or indirectly to make the administration viable,
(c) To devise ways and means to improve the working atmosphere of the department,
(d) Implementing the plans and programmes of the organisation,
(e) With his skill and experience he has to give proper guidance and instructions and also elicit his expert opinions for the benefit of the organisation,
(f) With his personality a Manager has to get jobs done by influencing others,

(g) A Manager has to check the progress of work of the employees under his control within the scheduled time,

(h) He should have the skill to solve problems.

Q.48. What is administration and what purpose does it play for an organisation?

Ans. Administration means the governance of any activity for straightening the irregularities and disorderly state of affairs as well as maintaining viability and system. Maintenance of sound and strong administration is very important for any organisation which wants to run trouble-free. Where administration is impaired and vacuous and/or weak, everything becomes messy and it quickens the degeneration of the organisation in all respects. For lack of administration no organisation can run smoothly and it leads to disarray. Therefore, maintenance of sound and strong administration in an organisation is immense. Sound and strong administration also attracts creamy candidates for employment.

Q.49. What are the probable reasons which lead to inefficient running of an organisation?

Ans. Probable reasons for inefficient running of an organisation are:

(a) Mass indiscipline amongst the employees which includes impunctuality in attendance, leaving the place of duty without permission thereby neglecting the duties entrusted with the employees, disobedience to the reasonable orders of the superiors and regular absenteeism,

(b) Lack of executive talent,

(c) Low output of work by the employees,

(d) Financial mismanagement,

(e) Faulty decision of the higher management,

(f) Defective planning,

(g) Reckless expenditure which can be curbed easily,

(h) Poor working condition,

(i) Dissatisfaction prevailing in the minds of the employees for unreasonable stiff attitude of the higher management,

(j) Sordid employee-employer relations.

Q.50. When the employees are at the height of their agitation over the issues not being fulfilled by the management, what course of action is left in such circumstances?

Ans. Demands of the employees backed by the Labour Union are insatiable and it is not possible on the part of the management always to mitigate their skyrocketing demands. Even after talking to the Union leaders across the table if nothing tangible comes out and they do not want to soften their attitude to come to terms in the matter of bipartite settlement of disputes, the only course left with the management is to give information to the Labour Directorate of the State Government by a letter apprising them of the prevailing situation. The Labour Directorate then seizes the disputes for conciliation and holds tripartite meetings for settlement over the charter of demands. The demands placed by the union leaders are then settled to the satisfaction of both the management and the labour union by the intervention of the Labour Directorate in the interest of maintaining peace in the organisation. If, however, there is no labour union in the organisation, the employees cannot be militant in attitude and their demands can be solved peacefully and easily by the management without referring to the Labour Directorate.

It is pertinent to mention here that in the event of tough and militant attitude of the employees and the union leaders, the management should not take recourse to declaring lock-out in the organisation, unless otherwise of course the situation goes beyond control in certain cases, in the interest of avoiding to sustain heavy loss to the organisation by such lock-out.

Q.51. Is it worthwhile that labour participation in the management will be helpful for smooth running of the organisations?

Ans. Industrial peace in most of the Indian industries is seriously disturbed which is adversely affecting production on account of discord prevailing between the management and the labour union. If labour participation is there in the management there will not be of course wrangling between the management and the union and hence the organisations will run trouble-free in the interest of attaining financial viability. This is no doubt one side of the advantage of labour participation in the management.

On the contrary, labour participation in management may lead to certain problems for the higher management, which may be as follows:

(a) When there is labour participation in the management, they will have the tendency to have upper hand and may dictate terms over the higher management which are likely to be contrary to the interest of the organisation as a whole.

(b) As far as appointment of new hands is concerned, the management may not have their own choice taking into account suitability of the candidates to appoint personnel but may have to accede to the request of the labour management for employment of such candidates even if they are not suitable.

(c) Labour participation in management means sharing of power in the running of the organisation. Accordingly, difference of opinion is likely to take place which may not augur well for the organisation ultimately.

(d) There may not be of course any immediate problem but with the lapse of time problems are likely to crop up with the consolidation of labour participation in the management.

Labour participation in the management is best suited in the case of such organisations which have lost viability mainly due to labour problems.

There are many organisations which are running most efficiently and without any trouble and the employees are very happy and are working with utmost efficiency.

In such organisations labour participation in the management is not felt a necessity.

Q.52. Is it recommended that there should be interaction between the superior officers remaining at the helm of affairs of the organisation and the staff members?

Ans. Yes, there should be interaction between the superior officers remaining at the helm of affairs of the organisation and the staff members, concept of working in establishments has completely changed in modern times. Master and servant relations are no longer there in the organisations. All employees, whether high or low, have to work in unison for the organisation and each and every employee has his own contribution to render for the development and prosperity of the organisation. If barriers are there between the superior officers at the helm of affairs and the staff members generating feelings of superiority and inferiority complex working under the same roof, sense of belongings to the organisation by the staff members will be conspicuous by its absence which will be an impediment for the development and prosperity of the organisation. Work will be speeded up if the staff members are given due importance and prestige—no matter their salaries may be much lesser than those of the officers of the company. Generation of oneness has to be created. Therefore, interaction between the superior officers at the helm of affairs and the staff members is essentially needed in consideration of the fact that all the employees are the members of the same family. By this, sweet and cordial relations between the officers and the staff members will also be maintained.

Q.53. What are the factors determining the remuneration prospects a candidate expects at the time of appointment?

Ans. While the quality and performance shown by a candidate at the time of interview are important determining the remuneration prospects, it also depends upon four factors, such as:

(a) market value (remuneration the candidate may get elsewhere), (b) replacement value (remuneration the employer may pay for the employee's replacement), (c) job value (the skill required for the job) and (d) contribution value (for the performance of the employee).

Q.54. Will it be in order if the female employees get lesser salary than the male employees?

Ans. It is definitely an unfair labour practice that there should be disparity in the salary structure of both male and female employees working for the same job. In India there is constitutional right to equality. While there is little remedy for the women employees if they get lesser salary than their male counterpart working in the non-governmental organisations, since the employees have to accept the employment on certain terms and conditions, in the case of public sector or governmental organisations women employees can institute action based on their constitutional right to equality, if there is discrimination in the matter of salary and other benefits amongst male and female employees.

Q.55. Can any employee refuse to carry out his transfer orders?

Ans. If the service regulation stipulates that the job is transferable, the employee has to carry out the transfer orders, provided the transfer of the employee has been necessitated arising out of exigency of circumstances. If, however, the transfer of the employee is with malafide intention of the management or when the transfer is effected in contravention of service regulation, the employee concerned can go to the court of law for redressal, but in this case the employee will start experiencing uncomfortable situation to work with the organisation, as the Management will not take in good taste of such behaviour of the employee. It is also the experience that the court does not interfere generally in the matter of transfer of employees, as the management is always ready to place convincing reason for transfer of the employees.

Q.56. What is outsourcing for an organisation?

Ans. In most of the large Indian and multinational Companies there is high salary structure for large number of junior and middle level employees. In cost effective and fluctuating economic situations these organisations generally do not want to have permanent liability of such high salaried employees and, therefore, go for outsourcing all lesser skilled employees from third party agencies for contract period of one or two years. The client organisations make monthly payment of salaries to these third party agencies who in turn give the same to their employees on pay roll of the companies after deducting provident fund and E.S.I. contributions. While making payment of salaries to the employees, the third party agencies of course take a cut of five to ten per cent of the employees remuneration. This outsourcing of employees is no doubt gainful for the organisations which have high salary structure for the junior and middle level employees, for the purpose of widening the activity of diversification.

Q.57. What is the distinctive function of Managing Director and Director?

Ans. The Managing Director has to play the role of Chief Executive. So, he has to perform those functions which are normally performed by the Chief Executive. He is the Director in one hand and Manager on the other. Whereas, an individual Director has no power and authority. He has to act collectively through resolutions passed at the meeting of the Board. He is the representative of the shareholders. Directors are the policy makers.

Q.58. Many industries are engaging casual labourers for doing certain job. But, the Labour Union is raising objection in many cases to the engagement of such casual labourers saying that by this engagement, the management is denying employment to the incumbents on permanent basis. Is this contention of the Labour Union correct?

Ans. Engagement of casual labourers is within the purview of the labour laws. If the job is not of permanent nature, it is within the right of the management to engage such labourers on casual basis. But, the management has to see that a casual labourer does not complete 240 days of work in a year to claim permanency in the job, for which he has to be paid off intermittently for a number of days, based on the fact that the job in which he has been engaged is not of permanent nature. If it can be established by the management that the job in question is not of permanent nature, the Labour Union cannot have any say in the matter and that they cannot pressurise the Management to employ such casual labourers on permanent basis. In such case, the contention of the Labour Union that the Management is denying employment to such labourers on permanent basis is void and not correct.

Q.59. Can a charge-sheeted employee engage a lawyer to defend himself in the disciplinary proceedings?

Ans. To all intents and purposes, management can throw out the request of the delinquent employee to engage a lawyer to defend his case. If the prosecution officer on behalf of the Company is not legally trained, the charge-sheeted employee cannot also claim to be defended by a lawyer as a matter of right. If, however, the prosecution officer is legally trained, the employee can also engage a legal professional to defend his case in the enquiry proceedings and in that case the management cannot have any objection.

Q.60. Supposing, there was no existence of Labour Union in an organisation. But, now all of a sudden the employees formed Union. What may be the possible reasons for formation of Union?

Ans. Formation of Union in an organisation is no doubt the democratic right of the employees. Indian constitution advocates trade unionism. Therefore, if the employees form union there is nothing unusual. But, at the same time a point arises under what circumstances they thought it prudent to form union in an organisation especially when the employees did not feel it necessary to think of forming union since inception of the organisation. The reasons for not forming union by the employees earlier were attributed to the following:

(a) Sweet and cordial relations between the employees and employers with interaction with the higher management,

(b) Treating the employees—whether high or low as the members of the organisational family,

(c) Job securities,

(d) Comfortable salary structure in consonance with the cost of living,

(e) Payment of profit sharing bonus,

(f) Congenial working atmosphere,

(g) Good behaviour from the management side.

If the employees start sensing that the outlook of the management towards the employees has been changing and the security and interests of the employees are being jeopardised as also the management has started becoming unreasonable towards the employees, they then find no other way out but to resort to form union as a means of guarding their interests. These are the possible reasons as to why the employees resort to form union.

Even when the employees have formed union, the management must always be benevolent towards the employees and maintain atmosphere of complacence in the minds of the employees so that they work with zeal. After formation of union by the employees, the management has also to see that they do not become militant in their attitude at any time.

Q.61. From the pragmatic point of view what should be the salary structure of employees?

Ans. Fixation of salary structure/gradation appropriately for different categories of employees is very important for any commercial house. In consideration of size and financial stability of organisation salary structure has to be determined so that net profit is not marginalised.

Most organisations of today are passing through cut-throat competition. Hence, in order to guard against such competition proper manning in the organisation is of paramount necessity. Irrational and baseless way of fixation of salary of employees has to be done away with. Also nepotism and favouritism must not be entertained while fixing salaries. There should not be disproportion in the salaries of the employees working for the same nature of job. Otherwise, it will foment displeasure and consternation in the minds of the employees which will not augur well for the organisation. Sky-rocketing salaries of the general categories of employees are not the solution to the attainment of efficient working of the employees, as has been observed in many organisations, as desire for increased salaries is insatiable. Salaries for different categories of employees should be fixed up in consonance with the present-day cost of living index as also the importance of positions in which the employees are engaged. If liberal fringe benefits depending upon the capacity of organisations are given to the employees, it does pay in the long run and the employees will be happy.

It is noteworthy to mention here that there should not be up-hill difference in the salaries of the high ranking officers as compared to those of other employees so as to avoid generation of feeling of mortification. If the higher management wants to satisfy the high ranking officers for the commendable job they have done, there are ample ways to appease them.

Q.62. If an employee submits resignation by serving one month's/three months' notice, as the case may be, in terms of appointment letter and the employer is refusing to release him, can he join his new assignment without acceptance of resignation letter?

Ans. Without acceptance of resignation letter which is submitted in terms of agreement/appointment letter, the employee can of course take up his new assignment and the employer cannot legally prevent the employee from taking up the new job. In such case, the management at least can withhold payment of dues of the employee till such time he hands over the charges. Release letter is also not mandatory unless otherwise it is demanded by the new employer. If, however, the new employer insists upon it which is most likely, the employee leaving the organisation can impress upon the erstwhile employer to issue the same (release order) and they have to issue it especially when the employee has submitted resignation strictly in terms of agreement/ appointment letter.

Q.63. Is it in order that the management could impose punishment to a delinquent employee on the basis of the findings of the Enquiry Officer in the domestic enquiry?

Ans. Domestic enquiry is a court where findings are arrived at to judge whether the concerned employee is actually at fault or not in the matter of charges levelled against him by the management. It is, therefore, perfectly in order that the management can act upon the judgement of the Enquiry Officer in awarding punishment to a delinquent employee if the charges are proved against him in the domestic enquiry. The Supreme Court has also laid down that where a disciplinary authority states that he has gone into the findings of the Enquiry Officer and agreed with the same, it is sufficient that the Management can go ahead with inflicting punishment if the charges are substantiated in the domestic enquiry conducted by the Enquiry Officer. There is of course provision that the aggrieved employee can challenge the orders of the management by way of a writ application in the appropriate High Court.

Q.64. If a labour court awards only 50 per cent of back wages to an employee who was reinstated from dismissal of his service on account of the principles of natural justice and that the dismissal was illegal, can he claim full back wages on his reinstatement?

Ans. The law is that the dismissed employee on reinstatement may not be entitled to get full back wages. The decision of the labour court to award 50 per cent of back wages depends upon the facts and circumstances of each case.

From the normality point of view, the high court will also not interfere with the quantum of back wages awarded by the Labour Court. If, however, the reinstated employee feels that it was unreasonable on the part of the labour court to award only 50 per cent of back wages, he can challenge the award of the labour court before the appropriate high court in its writ jurisdiction.

Q.65. While it is mandatory that any public sector establishment shall have to notify to the appropriate Employment Exchange for sending candidates other than managerial and the like for filling up vacancies, is it a compulsion that such candidates are to be appointed?

Ans. It is of course mandatory under Sections 4(1) and 4(2) of the Employment Exchanges (Compulsory Notification of Vacancies) Act, 1959 that before filling up any vacancy, any public sector establishment shall have to notify to the appropriate Employment Exchange mentioning the post, salary and qualifications, to send suitable candidates for interview and filling up vacancies. But, at the same time, Section 4(4) of the said Act clarifies that the employers are under no obligation to appoint candidates sent by the Employment Exchange, if they are not found suitable for the posts. They (employers) should of course intimate the Employment Exchange as to whether the candidates sent by them have been appointed by them or not. As far as non-employment of the candidates from Employment Exchange, the Apex Court clarified the position in the case of Union of India *vs.* N. Hargopal (AIR 1987 SC 1227).

Q.66. In some of the companies if the juniors are promoted in higher positions superseding the senior staff members in spite of the existence of merit-cum-seniority promotion scheme in the Company, could the senior employees with long working in the organisation not getting promotions go to the court of law for discriminatory policy of the management in the matter of promotion?

Ans. The decision concerning promotion primarily rests with the superior authorities and courts seldom interfere in the decisions on promotions. Therefore, it will be a difficult case for the employees not getting promotion to move the court. There are ample cases that many employees have attained seniority by virtue of long working in the organisation but they have no merit to work in higher positions. In such case, since they do not have both merit and seniority, the management cannot take the risk of promoting such employees. Under the circumstances, the management has to consider such employees for promotion who have proved meritorious although they are junior to others, especially when the promotion of an employee is felt an immediate need. Otherwise, the management has to maintain the merit-cum-seniority promotion scheme.

Q.67. When an employee is reverted as punishment for the offence committed by him, is it worthwhile that his salary has to be reduced for the lower position?

Ans. It will not be in order to reduce salary on account of demotion of the employee for the reason that the financial benefits which he was getting during the time of his erstwhile position are not curtailed. But while granting him annual increment, after allowing fitment, if it is felt necessary, the rate of increment should be in line with the graded increment for the position he holds after demotion. If, however, his salary has reached the last stage of the gradation of the demoted position, he should not be allowed any increment *i.e.*, there will be sealing in his salary till such time he is in the demoted position.

Q.68. If a dispute is taken up by an aggrieved employee with the appropriate authority under the Industrial Disputes Act, 1947 and in turn the dispute is referred to the State Industrial Tribunal, what is the maximum time limit to pronounce its award?

Ans. Section 10(2A) of the Industrial Disputes Act, 1947 provides that the order referring an industrial dispute to a tribunal shall specify the maximum time limit upto three months for announcement of award by the State Industrial Tribunal provided such dispute is connected with an individual workman. But, the Tribunal has the power to extend the time limit beyond three months on application made by any of the parties, if the Tribunal considers it expedient to do so.

In this connexion, it will be noteworthy to mention here that if the employee is dismissed from service or otherwise for which he is not getting salary/subsistence allowance, he can apply to the Tribunal for directing the Company to pay interim allowance to him till the award is pronounced, equivalent to the subsistence allowance as admissible under the Payment of Subsistence Allowance Act, 1969.

Q.69. After an employee quits employment of an organisation, can the erstwhile employer institute disciplinary proceedings against that employee on corruption charge or the like?

Ans. When an employee quits employment of an organisation there is no longer the existence of employee-employer relation and hence the employer does not have any *locus standi* to institute disciplinary proceedings against the ex-employee, as the charges, if there were any against the said employee, were not detected by the employer before he was released from employment. If the disciplinary action is still instituted after release of the employee, he can always approach the court for quashing the same. It may, however, be noted that the erstwhile employer at best can institute some other independent legal action against the ex-employee, even if he is not the employee of the organisation.

Q.70. When a petition is filed by the Management in the Hon'ble High Court for winding-up of a Company, can the employees intervene in the winding-up application and put their case before the Hon'ble High court to protect their interest?

Ans. It was clarified by the Hon'ble High Court of Calcutta in the year, 1983 in the case of National Textile Workers' Union, that the workers of a company could appear at the hearing of petition for winding up of the company. But, once a winding-up order becomes final, the workers will have no right to participate in any proceeding in the course of winding-up of the company. However, if aggrieved by the order of winding-up, the employees are entitled to prefer an appeal in the Hon'ble High Court.

Q.71. Under what circumstances an employee could be placed under suspension while issuing him a letter of charge-sheet?

Ans. In point of fact, service rules of an organisation provide for suspension of employees under the following circumstances:

(a) When an employee commits grievous offence for which his attendance to duties is pernicious pending finalisation of the disciplinary proceedings, he is placed under suspension while issuing him letter of charge-sheet.

(b) Suspension order can also be issued as a penalty for offence of serious nature committed by an employee.

The suspended employee is entitled to suspension allowance equivalent to one-third of his salary so long as he remains suspended. Such employee is also asked to report in person to the concerned official daily during the period of suspension.

Q.72. It may so happen in the office that an employee working under a departmental head is not allotted any work by him thereby putting him practically without work for which the employee starts feeling humiliated in the eye of others, which is the result of some hitch developed with his departmental head. In such case, can the employee take legal recourse to get out of this impasse?

Ans. As far as employee-employer relation is concerned, it is entirely the discretion of the departmental head to distribute work. If an employee is not allotted work and he continues to get salary, as usual even if he is sitting idle in the office, he does not have any recourse left for him to redress his grievances against the departmental head.

On the issue of humiliation the concerned employee should try to sort out the problem through discussions with the HRD personnel or the higher management.

Q.73. While accepting the letter of an employee for voluntary retirement by the Management, stating that the release order would follow shortly, can the employee withdraw the said letter before he is finally released under V.R.S.?

Ans. The Supreme Court of India clarified that the relationship between the employer and the employee is not terminated by the mere acceptance of the application for voluntary retirement till such time the employee is actually released from service against release order subsequently issued by the Management after the acceptance of the letter of the employee. Under the circumstances, the employee could withdraw his application although the same (application) was accepted by the Management but not released from service under VRS by the release order.

Q.74. Can the employer of an organisation deny payment of gratuity to an employee dismissed from service on ground of moral turpitude and/or fraud/financial irregularities?

Ans. It is the usual norm that gratuity payment is made to an employee at the time of leaving the employment either on retirement or resigning after completion of five years of service, in acknowledgement of the unblemished services rendered by him to the organisation. Therefore, if an employee is dismissed from the services of a company on ground of moral turpitude and/or fraud/financial irregularities, he is debarred from the entitlement of payment of gratuity, because his services under such circumstances are not free from blemish.

Q.75. In the event of death of an employee working in harness in an organisation, can the widow or the son, as the case may be, legally claim employment in the organisation?

Ans. It is not obligatory on the part of the organisation to accommodate the kin of an employee dying in harness unless there is rule providing employment in such case. However, on humanitarian ground the employer may consider providing employment to the kin of the deceased. There have been of course several decisions of the Supreme Court exonerating the employer from the obligation of giving compassionate employment.

Q.76. In many organisations appointment letters incorporating therein the complete terms and conditions of employment are not given to the selected candidates before they join duties but after a few days of joining the organisation—Why?

Ans. It is the bitter experience of many organisations that if appointment letters incorporating therein the complete terms and conditions of employment are issued to the selected candidates before they join duties, they in most of the cases do not report for duties even after getting the appointment letters in hands for the very specific reason that such appointment letters become the bargaining point with other organisations to get employment on higher salary and other advantageous terms and conditions. In such circumstances, the organisations issuing appointment letters in advance are debarred from getting the services of such selected candidates. Therefore, many organisations resort to the stratagem of not handing over appointment letters to the candidates before they join duties, although the same are kept ready, but issue simple and informal letters of appointment asking them to report for duties.

Q.77. Is it advisable to consider giving appointment to candidates who were once working/are presently working with the competitors?

Ans. Organisations should avoid giving appointments to the candidates who were once working/are presently working with the competitors for the very specific reason that such candidates generally continue to maintain cordial and informal relationship with their erstwhile employers and hence there is risk always that there is every likelihood that they may pass on secret information of the Company to them, if they are appointed.

Therefore, such employees may be harmful for the organisation and so they should not be considered for employment in the organisation even if they are found quite competent in the interviews.

Q.78. Can the employer reduce pay of a contractual employee during the period of his contractual service on some extraneous circumstances?

Ans. The answer is 'No.' It will not be in order to cut pay of a contractual employee during the period of his contractual service, under any circumstances, especially when the quantum of remuneration a contractual employee gets is specified in the agreement for contractual employment. In the agreement there must not be mention of pay cut in any of the clauses.

However, the other issue relates to dispensation of his service even before he completes full term of contractual service. Normally, in all the present-day employment contracts there must be mention of exit clause, permitting both the employer and the employee to opt out without giving any reason, after putting the other party on notice either for one month or three months, as mentioned in the agreement for contractual service. Therefore, the employer can at best terminate the contractual service in terms of the agreement instead of resorting to pay-cut.

Q.79. When a head of a particular branch is transferred to another unit of an organisation in the same position, he may be required to work there under his superior. Is it humiliating for him or derogatory to his official status?

Ans. By working under a superior in another unit on transfer, it does not speak of the derogation of official status of the official when there is no dwindling of his rank. An official may be the supreme head of a unit before transfer of his services which have been necessitated arising out of exigency of circumstances, but it does not mean that there will not be any superior official than him in the unit where he would be transferred. Transfer of his services should not be considered as punishment particularly when he has not been demoted, but transfer of his services has been necessitated in the broader interest of the organisation.

Q.80. For the purpose of guaranteeing the social securities of the employees, how many legislative enactments are there in India?

Ans. For guaranteeing the social securities of the employees working in different organisations, the following legislations are there:

(a) Workmen's Compensation Act, 1923,

(b) Employees' State Insurance Act, 1948,

(c) Coal Mines Provident Fund, Family Pension and Bonus Act, 1948,

(d) Employees' Provident Fund and Family Pension Fund Act, 1952,

(e) Industrial Disputes (Amendment) Act, 1956,

(f) Maternity Benefits Act, 1961,

(g) Payment of Gratuity Act, 1972.

Q.81. What are the services required for labour welfare and social security in an industrial organisation?

Ans. The services are:

(a) Latrines and urinals,

(b) Washing and bathing facilities,

(c) Creches,

(d) Rest shelters and canteens,

(e) Arrangements for drinking water,

(f) Arrangements for prevention of fatigue,

(g) Health services including occupational safety,

(h) Administrative arrangements within a plant to look after welfare,

(i) Uniforms and protective clothing and

(j) Shift allowance (for night shift).

Q.82. What are the obligations on the part of the employers to provide for in the factories as per the Factories Act?

Ans. The Factories Act makes it obligatory on the part of the employers to provide for the following:

(a) Rest room and a suitable lunch room in all establishments employing 150 workers or more,

(b) One first-aid box for every 150 employees,

(c) Cool and clean drinking water, latrines and urinals and washing as also bathing facilities,

(d) Canteen in establishments which employ more than 250 workers,

(e) Creches in factory establishments employing more than 50 women.

The Factories Act, 1948 stipulates that the factories employing 500 or more workers have to appoint a Labour Welfare Officer to look after the welfare of the workers.

Q.83. After suspension order is lifted from an employee on being acquitted from the charge levelled against him, is he not entitled to get full salary and other benefits during the period of his suspension?

Ans. It is not in order that full salary and other benefits would not be paid to an employee during the period of his suspension on his resuming duties after he is acquitted from the charge levelled against him. In this connexion, it is to be noted that the Supreme Court of India gave a ruling in a case reported in AIR 1984 SC 380 that the concerned employee was entitled to full salary and other benefits, as usual during the period of his suspension, after he was exonerated from the charge levelled against him. Usually, 1/3rd of salary is paid to an employee during the period of suspension as subsistence allowance.

Q.84. If a candidate is over-qualified can he be denied employment for the post he has applied, on this score?

Ans. Denial of appointment to a candidate who is over-qualified for the post beyond the stipulated academic qualification as required for the said post is irrational, arbitrary and unrealistic. Higher qualification cannot be a disqualification of the candidates to get employment than what is mentioned in the advertisement. The Apex Court has also held that the candidates cannot be shut out for employment for the post having higher qualification than the qualification required for a particular post.

Q.85. What are the criteria by which employees get job satisfaction?

Ans. Job satisfaction is a very important factor which leads employees attaining their efficiency in working and the organisation in turn is also benefited much by getting the efficient services of the employees. Hence, job satisfaction has dual advantages. There are number of important factors by which employees can get job satisfaction. They are—congenial atmosphere in the office, cordial relationship between the management and the employees, standardisation in the salary structure compatible with the cost of living index and the paying capacity of the organisation, right job for the right employees, allowing attractive fringe benefits depending upon the status of the organisation, so that the employees are devoted to work which will breed work culture and the management should read the pulse of the employees to know the reasons for their discontent in working, if any. A successful Manager has to see that the above are implemented in the broader interest of the organisation.

Q.86. Should there be any privacy for an employee in the workplace?

Ans. If any employee during the course of his working in the workplace wants to maintain his privacy in the case of mails, e-mails, phone calls, etc. which include his private communications and in such case if the employer wants to monitor the same, the employee is debarred from taking recourse to law to protect himself from such privacy, because there is indeed no right to privacy in the workplace. In fact, there is no statute in India that treats 'privacy' as a protectable right for an employee.

Q.87. What are the prime reasons for the labour discontent in Organisations?

Ans. In the earlier ages the relation between the Management and the employees/workers was like that of master and servant relation. But, this concept has now radically changed to employer-employee relation and naturally by this concept the employees deserve fair deal from the Management on all matters. Labour discontent breeds out of the actions of the Management such as :

(a) Depriving the employees/workers from paying them the actual profit sharing bonus,

(b) Depriving them from payment of double overtime as per law,

(c) Engaging them on longer hours of overtime work in contravention of labour laws,

(d) Unfortunately, for some reason or the other the relationship between the labour and the management has not always been in proper way,

(e) Frequent termination of the employees/workers who are on probation, as per the whims and caprices of the management,

(f) On account of wrong labour policy of the management,

(g) Dealing with the employees/workers with iron hand by the management on all matters,

(h) Discourteous attitude of the Management towards its employees/workers,

(i) Extracting work from them under incongenial circumstances,

(j) Discrepancy in the salary/wages of the employees/ workers doing the same nature of job.

Q.88. What is pen-down strike?

Ans. Pen-down strike is a disciplined way of resorting to silent agitation by the employees against the anti-labour policy of the Management. Employees also go for pen-down strike when they are dissatisfied with the inconsistent attitude of the Management staff towards the employees. Pen-down strike is a pointer to the Management that they should deal with the employees in such a way that there is no deterioration in the employer-employee relations in future in the interest of efficient running of the establishment by safeguarding the interest of the employees.

Q.89. What is the difference between salary/wages and remuneration/emoluments?

Ans. Salary/wages is that amount only which is paid to an employee for the services rendered by him in a month. This amount excludes any other financial benefits. On the other hand, remuneration/emolument is that amount which includes overall financial benefits an employee gets in an organisation for the services rendered inter alia salary/wages. Therefore, the amount of remuneration/emolument is much more than the amount of salary/wages,

Q.90. An organisation may have the presence of 2/3 or more labour Unions with different affiliations. All of them are claimants to be recognised by the Management. Under the situation, to which Union the Management has to recognise for the purpose of holding discussions on varied labour matters.

Ans. Although there may be the presence of 2/3 or more Labour Unions in an organisation, it will not be in the fitness of things on the part of the Management to recognise all of them for the purpose of holding parleys pertaining to labour matters of the organisation. In such circumstances, the management has to recognise any one of the Unions, who has the maximum number of employees/workers under its fold. In order, therefore, to gauge the exact number of employees/workers belonging to each Union, the Management has to invite lists from the individual unions mentioning therein the number of employees/workers under their signatures against their names who owe allegiance to such Unions. On scrutiny of such lists produced by the Labour Unions, the Management has to recognise that Union only who has the maximum number of employees/workers under its fold. While recognising the Union, the Management will call all the union leaders together and intimate to them its decision of recognition. The Management will also make it clear that while negotiating/settling issues of labour problems/disputes with the recognised union, it will be binding on the other Unions who have not been recognised and such Unions will give undertakings in writing to the Management expressing their assent in the matter of settlement of disputes with such union.

Q.91. Under what circumstances, transfer of an employee could be malafide.

Ans. Transfer of services of an employee is a condition of service which is also stipulated in the letter of appointment. If the service rules provide for transfer for administrative reason, the employee has nothing to do against such transfer and he has to comply with the transfer orders. If, however, service rules or appointment letter specifies that the employment is location-based, in such case the transfer orders of an employee could be termed as malafide. In this connexion, it is pertinent to mention that class-iv employees (white colour employees) are not to be transferred for administrative reason. Even if the services of such category of employee is required at the other end, local hands are to be appointed.

Q.92. Taking advantage of the squeeze in the employment scenario should the employers utilise the services of their employees in whatever manner they like?

Ans. Under no circumstances, it augurs well to utilise the services of the employees derogatory to their official status. There are plenty of cases that the employees are being utilised by the employers in contravention of their job profile which is the sequel to the dismal job situation. This attitude of the management is parochial and not a healthy sign for the organisation to prosper as the prosperity of an organisation is correlated to the complacence of the employees. It is not desirable that they continue to work with dissatisfaction if they are not given due weightage to the dignity of working. An enlightened management must not nurture perception that the employees could find little opportunity to get job elsewhere for squeeze in the employment scenario and hence should not extract work from them in whatever way they like by reducing the strength of the employees in the department than what is actually required. Otherwise, there is every possibility that this will give birth to the formation of labour union in the organisation where the strength of employees permits for the same (formation of union).

Q.93. Can an employee against whom domestic enquiry is conducted challenge that the Enquiry Officer was biased and that the enquiry was not conducted impartially?

Ans. An employee is always within his legal right to challenge the unfairness of the enquiry and that can approach the court of law to direct fresh proceedings to be conducted through another enquiry officer. But in this case, he has to substantiate that the enquiry as a whole was not conducted in a fair manner for which the employee has to take the following actions:

(a) It is of course a fact that proving bias of the enquiry proceedings before the court of law is difficult but still then the employee can establish some definite factual basis from which such bias could be substantiated.

(b) Mere allegation of the employee that the enquiry officer is partial in conducting enquiry and that he is biased against him (employee) will not be a valid ground in favour of the employee. In such case, the employee has to take objection against conducting the enquiry by the enquiry officer at the threshold and that the employee has to present the facts before the court of law that the enquiry officer was not impartial in conducting enquiry.

The Management should, therefore, ensure that the enquiry is conducted impartially so that the employee does not get any opportunity to go to the court of law to challenge the unfairness of the enquiry.

Q.94. Can organisations undertake compulsory retirement of employees leaving option to the employees concerned to challenge the same?

Ans. Compulsory retirement scheme can be implemented by the organisations if service rules provide for the same or otherwise an administrative order in respect of rationalisation of the organisations exists. Moreso, the current trend of the decisions of the Supreme Court of India is that an employee has little scope to challenge the orders of the organisations implementing compulsory retirement scheme. Under the circumstances, employers have wide discretion to identify the employees for dispensation of their services either on ground of rationalisation scheme of the organisation or otherwise there is the existence of service rules to this effect, leaving no option to the employees to challenge the orders of the management for dispensation of their services on the above counts.

Q.95. Is it not discriminatory if difference in retirement age between the management staff and clerical staff is maintained in an organisation?

Ans. It is not necessary that uniformity in the retirement age of clerical staff and that of the management staff in an organisation has to be maintained. Hence, it is not at all a discrimination if difference exists in the retirement age between the above two categories of employees in an organisation. It will of course not be in order if there is differentiation in the retirement age of the same category of employees. The Supreme Court of India has also upheld that officers of the management staff and clerical staff are not of the same category of employees and hence difference in the age of retirement of the two different categories of employees is not unreasonable and is permissible within the precincts of law.

Q.96. Is it obligatory on the part of an employee to obtain permission from the appropriate authorities of an organisation for prosecuting higher studies?

Ans. If there is a condition in the service rules of an organisation that the employee has to obtain permission from the appropriate authorities for prosecuting higher studies he has to abide by the same so as to enable him to be eligible for one step increment in addition to his usual increment or promotion, as the case may be, when he will be successful in passing the examination.

In defiance of this service condition if the employee does prosecute higher studies, which in other ways means without the knowledge of the higher management, such employee is obviously debarred from getting one step higher increment or promotion and he cannot legally claim the same.

However, in absence of service rules to this effect in any organisation, it is not of course obligatory on the part of an employee to obtain permission for prosecuting higher studies during the course of his employment; but it is desirable to seek permission from the management to improve his academic qualification which will pave the way in strengthening his case for higher increments or promotion in the organisation in future.

